Injecting Incentives Into the Solution of Social and Environmental Problems:

Social Policy Bonds

Injecting Incentives Into the Solution of Social and Environmental Problems:

Social Policy Bonds

Ronnie Horesh

iUniversity Press

San Jose New York Lincoln Shanghai

iUniversity Press
an imprint of iUniverse.com, Inc.

For information address:
iUniverse.com, Inc.
5220 S 16th, Ste. 200
Lincoln, NE 68512
www.iuniverse.com

ISBN: 0-595-15374-7

Printed in the United States of America

Introduction

This book introduces a new financial instrument, Social Policy Bonds, whose purpose is to make government spending more focused and cost-effective. That this would be a useful thing to do I try to show in the first two chapters.

Chapter 1 argues that achieving value for taxpayers' money is important. It points out that the size of government spending in the developed countries is large—around 46 per cent on average of total income in the developed world—and that in absolute, and even in relative terms as a proportion of GDP, it is rising. In this book, references to taxpayers' money should generally be taken to mean all funds that government compulsorily takes from its citizens. All levels of government—supranational, national and local—are included.

Chapter 2 argues that much government spending is misdirected, that it does not go to those most in need, and that it is wasteful or, even worse, counterproductive. Readers who are already convinced that government spending wastes a significant proportion of taxpayers' money can skip these two short chapters, and jump straight to Chapter 3.

In Chapter 3 I introduce Social Policy Bonds, a new financial instrument that would that inject market incentives and self-interest into the achievement of social goals. Chapter 4 looks at some of the practical aspects of a Social Policy Bond regime, and at how a transition to such a regime can be managed. In Chapter

5 I look at the advantages of Social Policy Bonds compared with the current policymaking process. Chapter 6 compares Social Policy Bonds with other 'more market' approaches to policy, while Chapter 7 looks at some potential problems of the bonds, and at political aspects of using the bonds in developed and developing countries. In Chapter 8, 'Putting it all together' I look at examples of current policymaking in the UK, and how a Social Policy Bond regime might remedy their deficiencies. Finally, in Chapter 9, I try to be realistic about what governments—even if they were to issue Social Policy Bonds—can and cannot achieve.

Chapter 1

Value for taxpayers' money is important

There are two main reasons for believing that it is important to get value for taxpayers' money.

- Because the sums involved are large and growing, and
- Because people are compelled to pay tax, on pain of imprisonment, and in liberal societies such an infringement of freedom should not be taken lightly.

Government spending is large and growing

Just how important is government spending? For our purposes, a useful measure is the government's share of national income, as measured by Gross Domestic Product (GDP). For the developed countries the current average is around 46 per cent. There are variations, but as Table 1 shows, the broad trend has been for this proportion to rise, despite persistent strenuous efforts to make cut backs and 'roll back the frontiers of the state'. It is also important to note that these are proportions of a GDP which was been rising rapidly—at an annual average rate of 3.7 per cent a year in the developed countries. Together these facts mean that government is spending a larger proportion of an expanding economy.

Table 1: General Government Spending as a percentage of Gross Domestic Product

	1960	1980	1990	1996
Austria	35.7	48.1	48.6	51.7
Belgium	30.3	58.6	54.8	54.3
Canada	28.6	38.8	46.0	44.7
France	34.6	46.1	49.8	54.5
Germany	32.4	47.9	45.1	49.0
Italy	30.1	41.9	53.2	52.9
Japan	17.5	32.0	31.7	36.2
Netherlands	33.7	55.2	54.0	49.9
Norway	29.9	37.5	53.8	45.5
Spain	18.8	32.2	42.0	43.3
Sweden	31.0	60.1	59.1	64.7
Switzerland	17.2	32.8	33.5	37.6
UK	32.2	43.0	39.9	41.9
US	27.0	31.8	33.3	33.3
Average, above countries	**28.5**	**43.3**	**46.1**	**47.1**
Australia	21.2	31.6	34.7	36.6
Ireland	28.0	48.9	41.2	37.6
New Zealand	26.9	38.1	41.3	47.1
Total average	**27.9**	**42.6**	**44.8**	**45.9**

Source: International Monetary Fund, published in The Economist[1].

Where does all this money go? There are four broad government expenditure categories:
- transfers and subsidies;

---

1. *The Economist*, 20 September 1997, survey 'the World Economy' (page 8).

- expenditure on government consumption: what the government spends on the resources it needs to supply services, such as health, housing, and education;
- interest on the national debt; and
- public investment.

In 1990, for the 17 countries in table 1, **transfers and subsidies** account for 22 per cent of GDP.[2] These include income support, unemployment benefits, invalidity and single parent benefits, and old age pensions. In the UK they now account for a quarter of the total economy—up from 14 per cent in 1960.

Spending on **public consumption,** such services as defence, law and order, education and health, is 17 per cent of GDP (in 1990) for the industrial countries. This is an increase from 13 per cent in 1960.

Interest on the national debt: this now amounts to around 4 per cent of total spending. it has risen sharply from about 1.5 per cent in 1990. This rise reflects the growth of government debt, caused by ever-increasing government deficits. It is government borrowing to pay for all its other activities. Deficits are the difference between what the government collects in taxes, and what it pays for all its activities. The interest is the interest on its borrowing.

For the developed countries in aggregate, government spending as a proportion of national income fell in only one of these categories between 1960 and 1990: **public investment.** This fell from 3 per cent to 2 per cent in those years.

Social Policy Bonds, which I will describe in Chapter 3, will address many, but not all, categories of this spending. They will,

---

2. This percentage figure, and those in the next three paragraphs are from *the Economist*, 20 September 1997, survey 'the World Economy'.

in my view, certainly make the supply of most services currently supplied by the state, more efficient. These will include health and education. Social Policy Bonds could be used to reduce crime and so may diminish the need for spending on law and order. In the developed countries listed in table 1, these services account for about 38 per cent of government spending.

Social Policy Bonds could also reduce the amount spent on transfers and subsidies, which together account for about 48 per cent of government spending. Much of this spending has an employment goal, but many of these transfer and subsidy policies have unclear or forgotten objectives. Social Policy Bonds may also reduce the need for unemployment benefit, and they would certainly reduce transfers and subsidies paid to industry.

I believe Social Policy Bonds would also make public investment more efficient. And overall, greater efficiency in this sort of spending would reduce budget deficits.

Government's share of Gross Domestic Product is not an infallible measure of the role of government in the economy, but it is useful as a rough and ready indicator to show that government spending is significant. We should also keep in mind that, in addition to direct spending, other forms of government intervention impose costs on citizens that keep them less rich than they otherwise would be. A prime example would be trade barriers, which keep the prices of imports high. These are a highly inefficient way of helping certain industries, or interest groups, who would not always be seen to be especially deserving recipients of assistance, if they were identified as such. Social Policy Bonds would do away with all such indirect interventions, and replace them with explicit, transparent, outcome-oriented policies.

There is a case for regarding a reduction of government spending as an end in itself (see next section). But Social Policy Bonds' main purpose will be to achieve greater efficiency and transparency of government spending, and I believe the bonds would do that. Once that is achieved, then I believe that government spending will fall, in both relative and absolute terms. That said, there are policy areas, such as the environment, where there is likely to be an increase in government spending. I believe this will happen regardless of whether Social Policy Bonds are introduced, but the fact that the bonds would be efficient and outcome-oriented means that government would be able to do more with its revenues.

Size alone means that it is important to achieve efficiency in government spending. There are other reasons. One is that in general, it is the poorest members of society who suffer most from badly designed government programmes. The poor rely more on these services than the wealthy. If they are working they suffer because high average tax rates tend to mean that they pay high marginal rates of tax—the so-called 'poverty trap'—which acts to discourage the unemployed from joining the work force.

When taxes are high, people make strenuous efforts to avoid paying them. This is both a waste of resources, and a loss of taxes. In the developed countries, the shadow (black, or underground) economy is estimated to vary from an additional 5 per cent of official GDP in the US and Japan, to around 23-28 per cent in Italy, Spain and Belgium—countries with a high tax burden.

These are pragmatic reasons for saying that government should get value for taxpayers' money. Are there others?

Big government is a threat to liberty

Many people view small government, however efficient or inefficient, as an end in itself. Democracy, these people would say, conflicts with liberty. There are no hard and fast rules in this area. Some would say that 'all taxation is theft', and rely on the voluntary sector to help those who cannot help themselves. Others would like government to show more evidence that the funds it exacts from its citizens are spent on strictly limited objectives, which it would be impossible, or very inefficient, to achieve in any other way. My own belief is that it is reasonable to say, as a society, that certain things, such as an at least adequate health care system and education system should be available to all; especially children, no matter how unfortunate or their parents might be.

Yet government involvement in the economy is far larger than would be required if its function were simply to assure this sort of safety net for all its citizens. There has been a gradual enlargement of the scope of government activity into more contentious areas. The private sector supplies an ever-expanding range of goods and services available for people, but government still suppresses, or discourages direct payment for such things as health services, primary and secondary education and some forms of insurance. Instead, government supplies these services, which are paid for by the taxpayer. There is no good reason for this. It is a situation that has evolved from the provision of such unequivocally beneficial public services as sanitation and lighthouses. This has happened largely through chance, or because government is itself one of many organised interest groups that have channelled resources away from the unorganised majority.

It is not necessary to be an anarchist or libertarian to have some sympathy for the argument that big government infringes on our liberty. This argument would be valid whether or not government spends our money wisely. But the pragmatic argument against big government is different. Government spending accounts for almost half our national income. The pragmatist wouldn't object to big government if we were getting value for our tax contributions. Are we?

Chapter 2

Is government efficient?

Some might think the argument that government is inefficient is self-evident. Government spending accounts for a third of the US income, for example, yet that country's inner cities are notorious for their 'poverty amidst plenty'. Readers in Britain, whose government spends around 40 per cent of national income, might ask why they still have poverty, long hospital waiting lists, rising crime, polluted seas and air, and rising homelessness. Few policymakers or commentators now argue stridently that these ills can be cured by raising the total amount of government spending, but individual sectors and interest groups still seek preferential treatment. Perhaps the best documented example of such an interest group (and one with which I am familiar) is the agriculture sector.

Taxing the poor to subsidise the rich: agriculture

Thanks mainly to research done by the Organisation for Economic Cooperation and Development (OECD), a Paris-based think tank, the effects of the panoply of government policies on the sector have been quantified, as have the costs to the people who pay for it.

Despite the sector's marginal statistical presence in the industrial economy, government support for agriculture is not trivial. In Britain, farming in 1998 contributed £7.2 billion to national income, but of this, it received £3 billion in subsidy from the European Union, and a further £700 million from the British Government. This means that farmers received more than half their income from taxpayers, and implies that the net production of the sector is about £3.5 billion. As one newspaper put it,[3] this compares with sales of paint worth £3 billion, or ready made sandwiches, worth £6 billion, neither of which are paid subsidies. The Common Agricultural Policy means that average European family pays 83 per cent more than world prices for its food, which costs the average family of four extra $1500 annually. On top of this, the average family pays another $400 each year as taxpayers.[4] In the OECD countries[5] as a whole, total transfers to the sector from consumers and taxpayers reached US$362 billion. This is about 1.4 per cent of these countries' total GDP.[6]

What is the purpose of this support, and has it succeeded?

Any hint that government might try to reduce its support to agriculture can be counted on to generate noisy and smelly demonstrations in opposition. Much of this comes from small farmers, who you might therefore suppose would be big losers if government left the sector to its own devices. In fact farmers as a whole receive few of the benefits from government support to agriculture. OECD research[7] shows that more than half of sums

---

3. 'Sandwich sales worth more than farming', *Sunday Times*, 26 September 1999 (page 2).

4. *Open Markets Matter: the Benefits of Trade and Investment Liberalisation, OECD 1998*, (citing a US estimate).

5. OECD members in 1999 comprise: all the EU countries, the US, Canada, the Czech Republic, Iceland, Norway, Poland, Korea, Mexico, Japan, Norway, Switzerland, Turkey, Australia and New Zealand.

6. *Agricultural Policies in OECD Countries: Monitoring and Evaluation, 1999*, OECD, Paris 1999 (table 1.5)

7. *Transfer efficiency of agricultural price support*, OECD, Paris, 1995.

paid out to 'agriculture' end up as extra expenditure on farm inputs, such as fertilisers, pesticides, animal feedstuffs, machinery and farm buildings. Farmers, because they are subsidised, buy more of these inputs, and the suppliers, knowing that farmers can afford to pay more, charge higher prices for them. There are also very high administrative costs as farmers have to comply with a whole host of stipulations to qualify for their assistance, and the masses of forms they fill in have to be duly scrutinised, filed, archived or otherwise disposed of. Criminals too benefit from the taxpayers' largesse: estimates are hard to come by, but one German criminologist who made a study of Euro-fraud, put the losses to the European Union at up to 10 per cent of its budget.[8]

Nevertheless, about 20-25 per cent of taxpayer and consumer support to 'agriculture' does end up going to farmers. But because much assistance to the sector takes the form of subsidised prices for their production, most of it goes to the farmers who produce most, and who you might think need support least. In the US, for example, 88 percent of support goes to the largest 25 percent of farmers, ranked by gross sales.[9] On average the proportion of the billions of pounds for agriculture in the rich countries that does go to the smallest farmers is about one quarter of one fifth, or five per cent. And many of these farmers are part-timers, who do not depend solely on agriculture for their income—in the US and Japan farming accounts for around one-sixth of the average farm's household income.[10]

---

8. Mr Klaus Tiedermann, quoted in the *New Zealand Herald*, 5 August 1994.
9. "*Distributional effects of agricultural support in selected OECD countries,* OECD document AGR/CA(94)27, OECD, Paris, 1994.
10. *A review of farm household incomes in OECD countries*, OECD document AGR/CA(94)27, OECD, Paris, 1994.

The big winners, then, from the complex array of agricultural support policies in Europe and other developed countries are: large farmers, many of whom were already very wealthy by any standards; agricultural chemical manufacturers; bureaucrats; and fraudsters. If these people had been explicitly identified as the major beneficiaries of such policies, it's likely they'd have been adopted less enthusiastically.

Consumers and taxpayers aren't the only victims of agricultural support policies though. Those who enjoy a pleasant rural environment are also lose. Farm subsidies have encouraged the decimation of wildlife throughout Europe. Market price support is still the main means by which the EU supports its farmers and it does so in ways that increase production per unit area. This increases the environmental burden on the land, and encourages specialisation of production. This puts pressure on food safety and animal welfare too. Both have deteriorated, as market price support encourages larger and larger units, and more and more intensive production.

Surprisingly many farmers have also, for the most part, suffered from the policies supposed to help them. Because of the way support has been given, it is largely capitalised into the value of farmland. So those who were lucky enough to land when these policies were first implemented benefited from a one-time windfall gain. As support levels have fluctuated, but mainly risen, over the years, so the value of farmland has fluctuated. High land values have meant that entry to the farming profession has been restricted to the wealthy or to the sons and daughters of farmers. But volatility of farmland values, largely a result of policy changes, rather than market fluctuations, has meant that those farmers who borrowed to buy land at the wrong time, have suffered. It is true that those who sold their land and left farming at the right time have done well. But most farmers, particularly those who enjoy their occupation and who are good at it, want to stay on their land.

There is a danger here of thinking that people within the rich countries have been the only victims of their agricultural policies. Perhaps these policies are an enlightened tool to help people in other countries? No it isn't. They maintain high prices partly by keeping out cheap food from overseas. So farmers and would-be food exporters in countries outside the developed countries suffer as they find that they are excluded from the world's biggest food consuming markets. They also find that these countries' subsidised overproduction has reduced the value of their output on world markets. Many would-be agricultural exporting countries are poor. The rich countries' agricultural policies hit them where it hurts—it makes development from an agricultural base that much more difficult. Agriculture, along with textiles and clothing, has been the traditional route for development of almost all the world economies, and it is precisely imports of these products that the rich countries do most to restrict.

In 1987 the (then) 24 OECD countries, many of them recognising the problems created by continuing high levels of assistance to their agriculture sectors, others perhaps pressured into appearing to do so, committed themselves to:

> A progressive and concerted reduction of agricultural support…; this will bring about a better allocation of resources which will benefit consumers and the economy in general.[11]

Since that declaration, which was reiterated in 1992 and in subsequent years, one salient fact stands out amidst all the agricultural policy reform packages introduced in many of these countries and the frenzied opposition to them: *overall there has*

---

11. *Agricultural Policies in OECD Countries: Monitoring and Evaluation*, OECD, Paris, 2000.

been hardly any reduction in support. In 1999, total transfers amounted to $361 billion: about $245 per man, woman and child in the countries involved,[12] and about $14,500 per farmer. This compares to $326 billion in 1987, when the OECD countries made their commitment to reduce assistance.

How did all this come about? One reason is that agricultural policies have obscure, unstated, uncosted or mutually conflicting policy goals. Consider the European Union's Common Agricultural Policy. Its supposed objectives, as laid down in the Treaty of Rome, are:

1   to increase agricultural productivity,
2   to ensure a fair standard of living for [farmers], and
3   to assure the availability of [food] supplies
4   ...at reasonable prices.[13]

A few minutes' reflection would tell us that these objectives conflict with each other. If agricultural productivity rises then the price of farm products will fall. Farm products are notoriously price inelastic; which means that as supply increases, then total revenue to the producers (farmers) will decline. So objectives 1 and 3 conflict with objective 2. The government, that is the tax-payer and consumer, step in to pay the difference. So consumers pay inflated prices, which are hardly 'reasonable' to those con-sumers who are much poorer than the recipients of all the CAP's support programmes. Equally basic an error is that no monetary values were ever put on achieving these objectives, so agricultural support has grown to swallow up about half of the European Union's budget.

---

12. *Agricultural Policies in OECD Countries: Monitoring and Evaluation*, OECD, Paris, 2000.
13. extracts from the Treaty of Rome (1957), Article 39

Is agriculture typical?

Agricultural policy in the developed countries has a longer history of government intervention than most other sectors. Its failures are well known and have been for many years. Most politicians and officials are fully aware that very little of the funds they spend on agriculture goes to those whom the original policies were supposed to benefit. Large amounts of it are wasted and much of the rest goes to the better off. As a result these policies have been widely challenged. Yet they persist. Policymakers have failed in their attempts to cut back, or reorientate agricultural support. Important reasons for this are that:

- cutting back on the most wasteful forms of agricultural assistance, including market price support, would mean not only falls in income on the part of a highly visible (and vocal) group, but also dramatic drops in wealth, at least in the short term. The value of most farmers' most valuable asset—their land—is underpinned by its ability to generate subsidies. Removal of these subsidies would mean great hardship for many farmers.
- the beneficiaries of this support include many of the people who make and administer policy. They have little incentive to withdraw or simplify assistance programmes, and are articulate advocates for the status quo.

Agricultural policy may not be representative of all government programmes in every respect, but the way in which its worst features persist despite their obvious defects is illustrative. And, as well, it is it is a significant expenditure item in its own right.

But is agriculture really untypical? What do we know about government programmes in other sectors?

Public expenditure in Britain

In *The Strategy of Equality*[14] Julian Le Grand examined the impact of public expenditure on medical care, education, housing and transport in Britain. His principal conclusion was that public expenditure, in almost all the forms reviewed, is distributed in favour of the higher social groups. Despite policy changes made since his study, which was published in 1982, the general features are still relevant. For major expenditure categories I summarise the largest categories of government spending, and Le Grand's findings.

Medical care

Government spending on: hospitals, community health, General Practitioners, dental services, pharmaceuticals, ophthalmic and central health services.

Findings: Le Grand found that expenditure per sick person is greater for the wealthier social groups. The wealthiest fifth of the population receive over 40 per cent more public spending than the poorest fifth. Doctors were also found to spend far more time on consultations with wealthier patients.

Education

Government spending on: nursery, primary, secondary and special schools, adult education and leisure classes, technical colleges, polytechnics and universities—all at that time largely free or heavily subsidised—plus tax relief for private schools.

---

14. Julian Le Grand, *The strategy of equality*: redistribution and the social services, George Allen and Unwin, London, 1982.

Findings: The wealthiest social group received nearly 50 per cent more public expenditure per person in the relevant age range as the bottom group. In secondary education the richest fifth of the population received more than 80 per cent more than the poorest fifth.

Housing

Government spending on: council housing at subsidised rents, rent rebates and allowances, payments to housing associations, improvement grants for home-owners, mortgage and other home-owner tax reliefs.

Findings: Apart from direct expenditures on council housing which do favour the poor, as also do rent allowances to private tenants, most other areas of housing expenditure are overwhelmingly directed at the rich, particularly tax reliefs for owner-occupiers, which have now ended. As a result, overall public expenditure on housing at that time favoured the better off, with the highest income group receiving nearly twice as much as the lowest.

Transport

Government spending on: Subsidies to British Rail (now privatised) and to bus, underground, and ferry services, grants for concessionary fares, provision of roads at no direct charge for use, tax relief on company cars.

Findings: Le Grand found that the principal beneficiaries of this spending was overwhelmingly the richest fifth of the population who, compared to the poorest fifth, received:

- nearly ten times as much subsidy per household on rail travel;
- seventeen times as much per household on private transport; and
- nearly four times as much per household on coaches.

Even subsidies to bus operators were found to benefit the better off, though not nearly to the same extent. Reasons for this are simply that the rich make more journeys and over longer distances than do the poor. They have more leisure time, and make greater use of commuter services. These make heavy losses, because they require trains and a complex infrastructure that are under-used outside the morning and evening rush hours. Professional households also use their private cars more: they make about three times as many journeys per person as semi-skilled and unskilled manual workers, and professionals also make greater use of company cars. While concessionary fares to pensioners tend to favour the poor, those to commuters favour the better-off.

The bias of government in its funding of transport is illustrative. Amongst lists of people who benefit from 'middle-class capture' of the benefits of government programmes, car-drivers rarely feature. Yet road systems the world over have been largely, and lavishly, built and maintained at taxpayers' expense. Taxpayers also contribute to the hospitals that look after the millions of people injured by road vehicles, and to the military required to ensure continued supply of fuel. Largely as a result of subsidised car- and truck- driving, any other way of moving around is either expensive or dangerous. So any attempt to introduce a rational road-charging regime is met by outcry. The effects of road subsidies on our physical, social and cultural environment have been incalculable.

As with transport, many seemingly neutral government policies tend to favour the long-distance at the expense of the local; the large-scale at the expense of the smaller. Regulations applying to food production, for example, are often aimed at mitigating the negative effects of large-scale production and specialisation. Yet they burden small producers disproportionately.[15]Again, the effects of government intervention on society are far-reaching.

In sector after sector a significant proportion, perhaps the majority, of government spending is not going to those who most need it. Much of it is captured by the better off, much is a pure loss to the economy. Government intervention for welfare purposes is at its most effective where it helps its poorest citizens; and helping the poorest members of society is, or was, often the implicit justi-fication for government involvement in supplying many of these services. Yet the most expensive government programmes appear to benefit mainly the middle classes. If people were told explicitly that the purpose of government involvement in health, education or transport or whatever, was to benefit the middle class, then it is unlikely that such interventions would continue. The point is not simply that this is over-government or deception, though these are issues, but that it would be far less wasteful and ethically more defensible if the government tries to help the poor and allows the better off to choose where and how they want to spend their money. All this is not to deny that there is excellence in certain areas: there are excellent state schools for instance, and excellent teachers within them; there are superb doctors and surgeons working in government-financed practices and hospitals. Even many farmers run highly efficient operations, given the perversity of the system within which they function. These people are not necessarily overpaid. The inefficiencies and misdirection of resources occur on a higher level and a larger scale.

The contrast with the private sector is instructive. The twentieth century saw expanding economic freedoms and an

---

15. See 'Lots of regulations, little effect', Chapter 11 of *Small is beautiful, big is subsidised*, principal author: Steven Gorelick, International Society for Ecology and Culture, Dartington, England.

ever-increasing range of consumer goods and services. But people in the developed countries have been forbidden, or discouraged, from choosing their own suppliers of such services as education, medical care or insurance for old age. Most people therefore don't have the bargaining power that comes with freedom of choice for these government-supplied services. In paying taxes instead, they suffer the worst of both worlds: they pay for a range of services that they may or may not want, but aren't allowed to choose who will supply those services. There are obvious incompatibilities with notions of political liberty, but our concern here is with efficiency. Simply put: there is no incentive for the suppliers of these statutory monopolies (or near-monopolies) to respond to demands for more, or higher quality, service. There are private sector alternatives available, but their costs to the taxpayer are in addition to those for which he or she has already paid. Government monopolies, even more than private monopolies, are free from the pressure to be efficient, or to innovate.

Why is the government so bad at doing things efficiently?

We should not be surprised that government is wasteful and inefficient. It didn't gain its 46 per cent share of our economies by being a preferred supplier. Its involvement in agriculture, for example, was happenstance. In Europe and many other developed countries it occurred as a result of war, and the need to boost food production and institute rationing. In many countries, its involvement in energy, post, telecoms, transport and some financial services were similarly haphazard. Its involvement in welfare, health, education, and provision for old age and unemployment also have little to do with its relative efficiency or being the preferred supplier in a genuine free market. In *The Dilemma of Democracy* Arthur Seldon argues that government tends to overreact to imperfections in markets such as those for education, housing and insurance:

> Government remedies are begun before the market imperfections have been removed by growing knowledge of [the market's] continuing flow of new, competing alternatives. They are applied too widely to where the market has not yet emerged, but could have been foreseen....And they are maintained long after they have become superfluous....[16]

And Seldon also points out that the '...evidence of history is that the imperfections of government are more deep-rooted and less remediable than the imperfections of the market.'[17]

In a competitive environment, companies that were as inefficient or wasteful as government would most probably lose business until they improved, or went out of business altogether. But managers in government operate in a different culture, in which results are not of overriding importance. Often, as we saw with the Common Agricultural Policy, policy goals themselves are unclear, inconsistent or incompletely specified. Many public sector managers don't have the autonomy of their private sector counterparts. Neither are they as accountable. So they rarely have the authority, or the motivation, to use resources in the most efficient manner.

In addition, controls on bureaucrats are seldom rigorous enough to prevent them pursuing their own interests—or the interests of the groups that have 'captured' them. These interests are often different from the elected ministers whom they are supposed to serve as agents, or the voters who elected these ministers, and whose taxes pay the bureaucrats' salaries.

---

16. Arthur Seldon, *The dilemma of democracy: the political economics of over-government*, Institute of Economic Affairs, London, 1998.
17. ibid.

Essentially these failings in the corporate culture of government and bureaucracy distill down to three:

- many government policies have objectives that are unstated, uncosted, obscure or conflicting;

- they reward activities or institutions, not outcomes; so that

- rewards to those involved in achieving objectives are uncorrelated to their effectiveness in doing so.

Government employees at all levels are human, and do have self-interest. Our task, I believe is to make sure this self-interest is congruent with the interests of those who depend on government for their essential services, and with the taxpayers who pay for these services. Social Policy Bonds, which I will introduce in the next chapter, aim to do just that.

Chapter 3

Social Policy Bonds

The previous chapters have shown, first, that taxpayer contributions to public spending in the developed countries are important and second, that taxpayers are not getting value for these contributions.

Government's performance is in striking contrast to that of the private sector—a contrast that is growing increasingly stark. Deregulation of western economies and freer trade over the past two or three decades have vastly increased the range and quality of affordable goods and services. At the same time the freer operation of self-interest in the private sector has made many individuals very wealthy indeed, and most income earners are better off. But the less well off and unwaged have gained little, at least in relative terms, and people from all backgrounds suffer from what they perceive to be a deteriorating physical and social environment. Many social and environmental objectives remain as remote as ever, despite large – and, in many cases, increasing—sums of taxpayers' money supposedly spent on their achievement.

The litany of social problems is familiar: crime rates remain high, while prisons are overcrowded; health services are plagued by too much demand and occasional scares. Many countries' state education sectors seem always to be in crisis. And environmental problems are a growing cause for concern. In continental European countries, in particular, unemployment remains high.

These problems differ from such concerns as wealth redistribution, which dominated political debate in the UK and elsewhere for many years. Nor are they similar to the ever continuing arguments about how to run an educational or welfare system. Such debates will never reach a conclusion. But high crime rates, illiteracy and water pollution, to give some examples, are problems that everyone agrees must be solved. Of course there are differences about how to solve them, and about relative priorities, but there is consensus that these are problems that deserve attention and some level of government funding for their solution. In other words, there is broad agreement over objectives, but little agreement over how to achieve them.

Many governments have privatised certain services previously done by national or local government employees. In many countries whole industries have been privatised, and this has undoubtedly been successful in increasing efficiency and increasing net returns to society. Central and local governments have contracted out services previously done by the public sector: in some US states, allocation of welfare benefits has been so contracted out; while in the UK, hospital laundries, and various other services previously supplied by local authorities have been similarly put out to tender. But the number and range of such contracting-out and privatisations should not obscure the fact that the volume of public spending continues to rise and, in most economies, so does government's spending as a proportion of national income. Government is still largely responsible for a whole host of services, transfers and subsidies and investment, and it is still performing badly.

The previous chapter suggested that likely explanations for the persistence of social problems, are the mis-stated or conflicting objectives underlying social spending, and the focus of such spending on activities, rather than outcomes.

I believe that these impediments to efficient achievement of social goals can be removed by injecting self-interest into the solution of social problems. The people who are currently charged with solving social problems are generally not stimulated or rewarded in ways that are correlated with their success in achieving social goals. This, I believe, is the fatal flaw that almost guarantees that the programmes of local or central government bodies will be ineffectual and expensive. These programmes reward people or institutions for undertaking activities, rather than for delivering desired outcomes. It is not that government employees are lazy or incompetent. It is that they don't operate within a system that rewards results. Government employees are behaving rationally given the incentives they face. They *are* self interested—the problem is that the incentives they face are only indirectly related to solving social problems. Their interests are not the same as those they are supposed to serve.

Inputs, outputs and outcomes

In discussing Social Policy Bonds, the distinction between terms inputs, outputs and outcomes is crucial.

Inputs   Expenditure, or those factors of production, such as staff, accommodation, other supplies, or other resources, that are used to produce goods and services. If we take fighting crime as an example, amongst the inputs devoted to lowering crime would be: police numbers; numbers of patrol cars; police spending.

Output   Things done or produced by people, such as number of reports produced and distributed, number of buildings constructed. Products that are directly attributable to the performance of an agency.

Outputs of a crime-fighting agency could be: numbers of police on the beat or on patrol at a time; number of police stations open 24 hours a day; number of toll-free phone lines; proportion of police emergency phone calls answered within 15 seconds.

Outcome   A set of circumstances, which is likely to be influenced by both an agent's outputs, and by factors outside agencies' control. Outcomes that might be targeted by crime-fighting agencies could be: a crime rate 10 per cent lower than in the previous year (as measured by number of reported crimes, or responses to victim surveys). The terms 'objectives' and 'goals' are used synonymously in this book to mean desired outcomes.

Social Policy Bonds

My proposal is that a new financial instrument be created that rewards people only when they actually achieve targeted social goals. A fixed number of Social Policy Bonds (SPBs) would be issued by local or national government and auctioned to the highest bidders. Government would undertake to redeem these bonds for a fixed sum *only when a specified social objective has been achieved*. The bonds would be freely tradeable after issue, and their market value would rise and fall. Social Policy Bonds would therefore differ from conventional bonds in that they would have an uncertain redemption date which, in combination with a fixed redemption value, implies an uncertain yield: holders would raise their bonds' yield by achieving the targeted objective quickly. The bonds would be redeemed with the government's general taxation revenue.

How would the bonds work?

Social Policy Bonds work because they create an interest group—bondholders—who have a strong interest in achieving the targeted social objective efficiently, or in paying others to do so. Consider an example. Assume that an urban authority is prepared to spend a maximum of say £10 million to reduce the crime rate within its borders by 50 per cent. It issues one million bonds that become worth £10 when the crime rate falls below 50 per cent of current levels for a sustained period—say one year. Because the market is will see this objective as unlikely to be achieved in the near future, it will put a low value on the bonds when they are floated. Assume successful bidders pay as little as £1 for the bonds. (This sum would be used by the authority partially to offset the cost of future redemption of the bonds.) Now, they hold an asset that could appreciate in value by 900 per cent if a sustained halving of the crime rate is achieved. This provides the motivation for bondholders to do what they can to reduce the crime rate.

What sort of problems can Social Policy Bonds solve?

In principle, any that can be reliably defined and quantified. Key criteria for policy areas within which Social Policy Bonds would show the most marked improvement over current programmes are:

1. existing policies have objectives that are unstated, uncosted, obscure or conflicting; and
2. financial rewards to those involved in achieving objectives are uncorrelated to their effectiveness in doing so.

Sadly, there are many such policy areas, including:
- crime prevention,
- employment,
- health,
- education, and
- air, water or noise pollution

How many bonds would be issued?

Before issuing the Social Policy Bonds, government would have to decide on the approximate value of the targeted outcome. One consideration is the financial impact of solving a social problem. Many social goals would actually bring about financial savings for the government. For each person taken off the unemployment register, for instance, the exchequer would save unemployment benefit, and receive an increase in income tax. In this instance, the net fiscal benefit of a social goal can be high, even in the short term. For some targeted objectives, such as a lower crime rate, there would also be positive, but less easily quantifiable, net financial benefits, and they may take longer to arise. Other social goals, such as reduced rates of homelessness, or increases in literacy, could increase returns to the government in the long term, but would bring about very little financial return in the short run. Targeting many social or environmental goals, though, would impose net financial costs on the government in the foreseeable future.

But government takes a wider view. People, and governments, want things other than for financial reasons. A society in which everybody can read, in which people feel safer from crime and breathe cleaner air is desirable in its own right. Government and society have to decide on how far we pursue these objectives, and how valuable they are. Do we aim for 95 per cent literacy or 100 per cent, for example?

Government would have to take into account both the financial and nonfinancial benefits in deciding on the maximum value of each social goal, in advance of issuing the bonds. If Social Policy Bonds are to be used in conjunction with other policy instruments to achieve the same goal, government would also have to decide what proportion of the total expenditure would be spent on the bond redemptions. These factors would determine how many bonds it would issue for a definite redemption value. The maximum cost to the government of the bond issue would equal: the total number of bonds issued multiplied by the redemption value *plus* administration costs *minus* any revenues gained on floating the bonds.

But while it has to decide on the *maximum* cost to society of achieving the objective, a government issuing bonds wouldn't have to work out how much the actual cost will be with any accuracy. That would be done by would by bidders for the bonds in the open market. Assume that Social Policy Bonds are to be used exclusively in pursuit of a desired social outcome, and that the government issues one million bonds, of redemption value £10. If the market decides that the issue value of these bonds is £1, the net cost of achieving the targeted objective (neglecting administration costs) would be £9 million. In other words, the market at the time of issue believes that the cost, including its profit margin, of achieving the objective will be £9 million.

But suppose the government is in the dark about how much it will cost to achieve a targeted objective and instead of issuing one million bonds, it issues 10 million with the same redemption value, £10.00. It would then be liable for a maximum cost of £100 million. However, the market will still reckon that it could achieve the objective for around £9 million. So instead of valuing the bonds at £1.00 it would bid up the issue price of the bonds to around £9.10.[18] The government therefore doesn't have to do all the work in deciding how much a targeted objective will cost to achieve, and it can put a cap on its total liability by limiting the number of bonds issued.[19]

The Social Policy Bond mechanism ensures that the market, which means people *other than government employees* decide roughly how much a targeted objective will cost to achieve. They will do this when they bid for the bonds at issue, and afterwards. This fact, and the would-be bondholders' incentive to minimise their costs, contrast with the current system, in which the costs of achieving particular outcomes, if they are calculated at all, are not widely known, nor subject to competitive bidding. Under the current system, in fact, many of the people involved in achieving social goals have every incentive to inflate the projected cost of their doing so.

Note that the government could add to the number of bonds in circulation after floating, at any time, if it wanted to boost the efforts going into achieving a particular social goal. If the government wanted, for whatever reason, to *reduce* such efforts, the situation is a little more complicated. The government could buy bonds back from holders, but doing so would reduce the total funds to be spent on achieving the targeted objective, and so would lower the value of all bonds in circulation. People may therefore be unwilling to buy bonds in the first place, if they thought there were a high probability of the government's buy-

---

18. Social Policy Bonds would be an unusual financial instrument, in that the more that are issued, the higher would be their value!

19. For most social objectives, the sums of money involved will be flows, rather than stocks, in that sustained achievement of the targeted objective is required, but the reasoning is the same.

ing some of them back in this way. They would demand some sort of premium for taking that risk. Or the government could undertake either that it would never buy Social Policy Bonds back or, that if it did, it would undertake to buy them all back at the market value ruling before it announced its purchases.

Who would buy the bonds?

Many people would purchase these bonds with the idea of doing nothing but holding on to them until they could sell them at a profit. These *passive investors* would have no intention of doing anything to help achieve the social goal targeted by their bonds. Some of them would be casual purchasers, who would buy the bonds with the same intent as they would a lottery ticket. They would hope to hold on to the bonds until redemption, or until their market value had risen sufficiently high for them to enjoy a worthwhile capital gain. Other passive investors would be speculators, who know, or think they know, that the likelihood of the objective being achieved quickly is greater than the rest of the market thinks it is, and that the bonds are therefore underpriced.

Another category of passive investor might be the hedger. These would be people who, in the absence of the bond issue, stand to lose if the particular targeted objective were achieved. Hedgers might buy the bonds as a form of insurance against this possibility. In the crime example, hedgers might be those who breed guard dogs, for instance, or who operate minicabs in areas where street crime is prevalent. Actually, though, the losers from particular Social Policy Bond issues might not be clearly identifiable in advance, because the bonds will not stipulate *how* a goal is to be achieved. So, bondholders might decide that one of the most effective ways of reducing crime is to subsidise the cost of guard dogs to home owners, which would *increase* demand for the animals.

Casual purchasers and speculators would want to become 'free-riders', hoping to benefit from any increase in the bond price without actually participating in any crime-reducing projects. Hedgers wouldn't particularly want the value of their bonds to rise, but their bondholding would similarly reduce the supply of bonds available to active investors. However, the way markets work would limit the opportunities for all these passive investors. The more bonds they collectively own, the more remote the targeted objective becomes, the lower the market price of their bonds will fall, and the more they stand to lose as the aggregate value of their bond holdings falls (see Box). At some point, then, it would become worthwhile for passive investors either to become, or to sell their bonds to, *active investors.*

These people, or institutions, would use their own capital, or borrow on the strength of the redemption value of their bonds, to initiate or facilitate crime-reduction programmes. Active bondholders would have an incentive to cooperate with each other to help reduce crime, and to do so as cost-effectively as possible. These people's motivation will come from the expected capital gain they will enjoy as the bond price rises with the enhanced probability that the objective will be achieved early.

The free rider question

One question often asked when I speak about Social Policy Bonds is whether 'free riders' could undermine the workings of the bond mechanism. Some people think that a significant number of purchasers of the bonds would hold them with no intention of doing anything to help solve the targeted social problem.

I don't agree that free riding would be a serious problem for a Social Policy Bond regime, partly because not much free riding would occur, and partly because even if it did occur it would not impede the operation of the bonds mechanism. I believe that free-riding would be a self-cancelling activity. If most of the bonds were held by would-be free riders, then little would be done to help achieve the targeted objective. It would become more remote, and therefore the value of the bonds would fall. As the bonds lose value, they would make a more attractive purchase for people who would be prepared to solve the targeted problem. And the free riders would be tempted to sell, even at a loss, rather than see the value of their bonds continue to fall. Some history of falling bond prices would tend to make free riding on Social Policy Bonds less appealing in the future. There are other reasons why free riding probably would not work with Social Policy Bonds:

- Individual free riders would have no incentive to collude with other free riders, because the more they did so, the more remote the targeted objective would become, and the further would the value of their Bonds fall. This would act so as to limit any free riding activity to small players.
- As with other financial instruments, small players would probably pay higher transaction costs than the bigger institutions—the ones that can do something to solve social problems.
- Small players also would not have access to the research that would enable big players to value the Bonds accurately. Therefore they would be at a disadvantage in the market.

Note also that even if free riders were to gain from holding Social Policy Bonds, it would happen only if the targeted objective were achieved, or became closer to being achieved. Attempted free riding could have positive effects: it could add liquidity to the Social Policy Bond market. And note that free riding needn't necessarily act as a disincentive to investors who are prepared to help solve the targeted social problem. Company executives, for instance, who don't hold all their company's shares, are hardly deterred from trying to maximise the company's sales and profits, even though passive shareholders also gain.

Hedgers, though passive purchasers of the bonds, would not necessarily be hoping for the value of their bonds to rise. Their hedging activity could reduce the incentives available to active investors. On the other hand, it could moderate their opposition to objective-achieving initiatives. Once Social Policy Bonds had been tried, it might be that futures and options markets would develop, further increasing liquidity, and giving hedgers the chance to leverage their insurance without withdrawing bonds from the supply in the market, to be bid for by would-be active investors.

What would bondholders do?

Continuing with the crime example, consider some of the measures that active investors in the bonds could put into operation:

- encouraging neighbourhood watch schemes;
- encouraging parents to monitor their children's activities more closely;
- subsidising recruitment of unemployed workers;
- complementing police patrols with private security patrols;
- subsidising widespread use of window locks or burglar alarms; or
- financing research into the causes of crime.

Many of these activities are, to some extent, undertaken by local bodies or some arm of government nowadays. Certain longer-term projects, like research into the causes of crime, are often done by private bodies or universities, independently of government or with a proportion paid for by government funds. The crucial difference is that, under a Social Policy Bond regime, people would have incentives to seek out and develop those ways of reducing crime that are most cost effective. A police force, a bureaucracy, or an environmental health department, however well-intentioned, is not rewarded in ways that correlate with its success in achieving society's objectives—even if these are explicit. But under a Social Policy Bond regime, the self-interest of bondholders acts so as to encourage those ways of reducing crime that give tax- and rate- payers the best return for their outlay. These ways may have been tried before, or tried in different cities, or they may be new and untried. Bondholders would be motivated to seek out, invent and use the most efficient methods for whichever city or country whose crime rate is targeted.

Of course, the bondholders need not participate directly in any crime reduction projects. Their role could be one of financing such projects, on the strength of the redemption value of their bonds, or on the strength of any increase in the value of their bonds. Their motivation arises from the anticipated supernormal profit arising from early redemption of the bonds.

One further activity that bondholders might indulge in is lobbying government. They may make the case for higher prison sentences, for example, because they think that would deter criminals. Such lobbying, of course, already goes on because government is always making decisions that create winners and losers. Under a Social Policy Bond regime, the source of this sort of pressure, and the motivation for it, would be more transparent than under the current system, and it need not pose any different problems. I shall say more on the subject of lobbying in chapter 4.

Trading the bonds

Social Policy Bonds, once issued and sold, must be readily tradeable at any time until redemption. The operation of such a 'secondary market' is critical to the way Social Policy Bonds work. Many bond purchasers will want, or need, to sell their bonds before redemption—which may be a long time in the future. With a secondary market, these holders will be able to realise any capital appreciation experienced by their holdings of Social Policy Bonds, whenever they choose to do so. This would make the bonds a more attractive investment in the first place.

Such capital appreciation would arise from upward movements in the market price of the bonds. Of course, prices of the bonds will move in both directions. Major determinants of the market price would be:

- how remote the market believes the targeted objective is to being achieved;
- the relative attractiveness of other investments; and
- market perceptions of risk and uncertainty.

All these, and other determinants, will vary with time. Note that the market's valuation of the bonds will be influenced not only by efforts that bondholders make toward achieving the targeted goal, but by external factors. Some of these could be known reasonably well by the market at the time of issue: for instance, one of the determinants of crime is demography. Specifically, the greater the number of young male adults, the larger the number of crimes tends to be, all other factors being equal. Demographic variables like this, and others that can be anticipated, would be factored into the market value of the bonds at issue. But other influences cannot be anticipated. So, for example, the market price of bonds targeting property crime could fall if, say, there were a string of power failures, leading to looting. Or it could rise on the capture of a ringleader of a major gang of burglars or car thieves. The price of bonds targeting air pollution could rise or fall with climatic conditions, volcanic eruptions, or the price of oil or coal. The value of bonds targeting unemployment could rise or fall with financial data, such as the exchange rate (making the country a more or less attractive venue for overseas investment), or interest rates (making firms more or less likely to lay off employees).

As with other investments, risk (quantifiable) and uncertainty (unquantifiable) would be important determinants of the bonds' market price. More remote objectives (cutting crime by 80 per cent say), being riskier as well as (probably) longer term investments, would sell for much lower prices, than those whose outcomes were closer to current levels (cutting crime by 20 per cent). And there would also be uncertainty attached to the Social

Policy Bond mechanism itself, especially in the early years of a Social Policy Bond regime, as it would be untried and unproven.

As with shares and other financial instruments, the prices of Social Policy Bonds would be in constant flux. New information affecting the prices would become available day by day. Much of the research used to generate this information, and the effects its release has on the bonds' market value, would give useful insights into the relationships between circumstances, events, social problems and desired outcomes.

Giving bondholders the chance to benefit from these price movements is essential. Apart from making the bonds more attractive at issue, there is another important reason for requiring a healthy secondary market in the bonds: active investors may be able to speed up only one, or a few, of the processes necessary for the targeted objective to be achieved. Once these investors have contributed what they can, and seen the capital value of their bonds increase in line with the increased probability of the bonds' early redemption, they may have no wish to speculate on the speed at which the remaining processes will be carried out. Other groups of active investors, who will have greater expertise in performing these later processes, must be given an incentive to use their expertise to accelerate attainment of the targeted objective. The possible capital appreciation of bonds bought from previous owners and sold at a still higher price (or redeemed) provides this incentive. The new owners will, if they are successful in these later stages, realise this capital appreciation.

It is this tradeability that is one of the features that differentiates Social Policy Bonds from other attempts made to privatise social services. Tradeability:

- avoids the problem of possible collusion (tacit or not) between bidders for contracts; under the current system, inflated bids can succeed if the bidders agree (explicitly or not) to inflate their bids. Under the Social Policy Bond system, the bonds could be bought and held by anybody, not just people already involved in carrying out the target-achieving projects, or well set up to do so. So the number of possible bidders is not limited to a few likely operators, but is open to all who are prepared to do, or to finance the doing of, things that will help achieve the objective. The fact that anybody can be involved in the bidding for Bonds at any stage, will discourage people from making excessive bids, so ensuring that social objectives will be achieved as cost-effectively as possible.

- encourages suppliers of services to continue to minimise costs and maintain efficiency, *after* they have started helping achieve the targeted goal. Under the current system there may be a tendency for contractors, or their employees, having won a contract, not to maximise the speed and efficiency with which they go about solving the targeted problem. While they can sometimes benefit from being efficient, they cannot always enjoy this benefit in terms of immediate cash capital gains. There is scope for incentive payments, or penalty clauses, but these are crude, ad hoc arrangements that are costly to administer or impose. Under a Social Policy Bond regime, if bondholders are unexpectedly efficient (or if external events make them so: lucky) they can sell their bonds and realise their capital gains before all the necessary work has been carried out. And if bondholders are inefficient, *they* are the losers, not taxpayers.
- transfers risk of breach of contract from the tax- or rate-payer to bondholders. If, under a contract system, the successful bidders fail to do what they were legally obliged to do, then it is up to the aggrieved party—the central or local government agency—to take proceedings against them.

Even if such actions are successful, they can be protracted and costly. Under a Social Policy Bond regime, underperforming bondholders will find a ready market for their bonds in people who believe they can be more efficient.

Cascading incentives

As the bonds are traded, they would tend to flow towards those who are most able to help solve the targeted social problem. In fact, though, it is not necessary for there to be any actual flow of bonds. Large bondholders might simply decide to subcontract out the required work to many different agents, while they themselves hold the bonds from issue to redemption. The important point is that the bond mechanism ensures that the people who allocate the finance have an incentive to do so efficiently and to reward successful outcomes, rather than merely to pay people for undertaking an activity. At the limit we can conceive of just one single buyer of all the bonds. If this buyer were determined to hold on to the bonds until redemption, then the bonds would function as a sort of performance-related contract, with the government paying only when the objective has been achieved. The buyer could contract out most, or all, of the work required to achieve the objective, with the incentives given by the bonds for speedy accomplishment cascading down from the bondholder to those subcontracted to do the work. If this bondholder, for whatever reason, were to become inefficient in pursuit of that objective, or were simply to lose interest in it, then s/he could simply sell the bonds to more efficient or motivated investors.

Too large a number of small bondholders would probably do little to help solve targeted social problems by themselves. If there were many small holders, it is likely that the value of their bonds would fall until there were aggregation of holdings by people or institutions large enough to initiate effective problem-solving projects. In much the same way as share privatisation issues the world over have turned out, the bonds would mainly end up in the hands of large holders—individuals or institutions. Between them, these large holders would probably account for the majority of bond holding. Even these bodies might not be big enough, on their own, to achieve much without the cooperation of other bondholders. They might also resist initiating projects until they were assured that other holders would not be 'free riders'. So there would be a powerful incentive for all bondholders to *cooperate with each other* to help solve the targeted problem. They share the same interest in seeing targeted objectives achieved quickly. So they would share information, trade bonds with each other and collaborate on objective-achieving projects. They would also set up payment systems to ensure that people, bondholders or not, were mobilised to help achieve targeted objectives. Bondholders would either trade bonds, or make incentive payments to ensure that any proceeds from higher bond prices, or from redemption, would be channeled in ways most likely to stimulate speedy achievement of the targeted objective. Large bondholders, in cooperation with each other, would be able to set up such systems cost-effectively.

Regardless of who actually owns the bonds, aggregation of holdings, and the cooperation of large bondholders, would ensure that people who are help achieve social goals are rewarded in ways that maximise efficiency.

Objectives and indicators

First, a couple of definitions: *social objectives* in this book, are the same as *social goals*, such as better health, education, and a cleaner environment.

Indicators are quantifiable measures, which can be used singly or in combination, to chart progress towards objectives. For health, longevity or infant mortality would be indicators. For a cleaner environment, air and water pollution levels would be indicators.

For the Social Policy Bond regime to be effective, the targeted objective, and its associated indicators, must be carefully defined, so that targeted changes either actually are, or are strongly correlated with, what society wants to achieve. For instance, numbers of reported crimes could be targeted, if the objective is to achieve a safer urban environment. But this indicator may be unsatisfactory if, for instance, the crime rate becomes so high that people don't bother to report minor assaults or burglaries to the police. A more appropriate indicator might be derived from responses to victim surveys. The bonds demand clear thinking as to exactly what it is that society wants to achieve. Do we want lower unemployment? Or lower expenditure on unemployment benefit? Or higher employment? Should we target unemployment amongst 16-24 year old males? Of racial minorities? Or in particular regions? Apart from making unemployment reduction more efficient, a Social Policy Bond regime would also clarify and make explicit, society's goals in this and other policy areas.

What are the desired attributes of objectives that make them suitable for targeting by Social Policy Bonds?

Objectives will have to be *carefully defined*, so that they achieve what society wants to achieve. Consider the objective of a lower crime rate. Clearly it would be unsatisfactory to redeem the bonds when crime was down by a certain level for a short time only. The objective will be a sustained lower level of crime, and this is how it would have to be defined when the bond is issued.

Objectives should be capable of being *targeted by quantifiable indicators*, whose progress accurately corresponds with progress toward the desired social outcome.

In general, objectives should be as *broad* as possible, so that a particular objective cannot be achieved at the expense of others.

The last point needs elaboration. As an example, consider the application of a bond regime to environmental problems. Assume the concentration of atmospheric lead were to be targeted in a bond issue. It might be that targeting lead in this way would cause people to increase their use of other polluting substitutes—and these could be more dangerous than the original levels of lead.

One way of dealing with this problem could be to aim initially at unambitious reductions in the lead level. Depending on the effects of this reduction on the use of offending substitutes, other bonds could then be issued, either targeting the level of lead, or targeting the level of the offending substitutes. But a better approach would be to target, more comprehensively, atmospheric pollution. This could be expressed perhaps as an index of atmospheric pollutants, weighted according to their lethality and other factors.

Similar approaches, perhaps less clear-cut, apply to solving regional problems. If bonds were issued targeting the number of unemployed people in north-east England, say, then people may attempt to solve the problem by paying the unemployed of that region to move somewhere else. It may be that this would be seen as a social benefit. But if not, provisos could written into the bond issue, such that they would not be redeemed if the population in the north-east fell below a certain level. Again, for the bonds to work, clarity and transparency as to what exactly is the desired social outcome are essential.

We shall see examples of objectives and indicators that are too narrowly defined in the Chapter 8, but for the moment we should note:

- that in general, objectives that are complementary and that, if not pursued jointly, could conflict, should be targeted by a single bond issue; and
- that the correct choice of quantifiable indicators is necessary not only under a Social Policy Bond regime: such indicators are of growing importance in conventional policymaking.

Chapter 4

Practicalities and potential problems

This Chapter looks at how to introduce, and manage a transition to, a Social Policy Bond regime, and how such a regime would interact with government and existing institutions.

Social Policy Bonds: interaction with government

Social Policy Bonds would represent a radical change in the way in which our society does things. At first sight, a bond regime may even seem outlandish: it appears to mean that government gives up its responsibility for achieving social goals to the private sector. But it is important to realise that under a Social Policy Bond regime government is merely contracting out the *achievement* of social objectives. Government still sets these goals and, by undertaking to redeem the bonds, is still the ultimate source of finance for the projects that achieve them. People will need to be reminded of these facts when asked to contemplate a bond regime.

They will also need to be reassured that government would not relinquish its existing sanctions against illegal acts. Social Policy Bonds work by giving financial incentives for people to achieve particular social goals. But they may also encourage people to break the law to do so.

Examples of acts that would be illegal, but that certain bond issues might encourage, are:

- forcibly preventing people from registering as unemployed, if bonds targeting unemployment are issued;
- emitting pollutants that, while unspecified in bonds targeting pollution, are still controlled or banned;
- falsifying data used to compile such health indicators as longevity or infant mortality.

Acts such as these are already illegal, and will continue to be so, but before issuing Social Policy Bonds, governments should be aware that there will be greater inducements to commit them.

The bonds will also induce people to modify behaviour in ways that, while not illegal, would undermine what they are trying to achieve. So, for example, if bonds targeting the number of reported property crimes are issued, bondholders might lobby insurance companies not to insist on police reports before paying out. Or they might persuade, or pay, insurance companies to raise their excess levels. Either activity would discourage people from reporting minor thefts. Neither would do anything to reduce property crimes, but they would each make the targeted objective, lower numbers of *reported* property crimes, more achievable, and so lead to a rise in the bonds' market value. Insurance companies themselves could own the bonds, and so it would be in their own interest to deter people from reporting property crimes. In this particular case, the objective could be more carefully specified so as to target not 'reported crimes' but, for instance, the number of people who say, in surveys of the public, that they have experienced property crimes.

If higher levels of literacy are targeted, bondholders may be tempted to lobby in favour of easier reading tests. Again, judicious specification of the targeted objective would help: the bonds could stipulate the exact reading test to be used, or that the test will be certified appropriate by a specified panel of impartial panel of literacy experts.

In general though, carefully specified objectives will not always eliminate or mitigate the kind of illegal, or negative-but-legal, activities that the bonds may stimulate. So how can this potential problem be solved? The solutions have to do with the way in which the bonds are introduced, and with the role of government.

Introduction of a Social Policy Bond regime

Social Policy Bonds will need to be introduced cautiously. They should be tried out on an experimental basis at first. Initial goals could be relatively small scale and uncontroversial, and the Bonds could complement, rather than replace, existing government or local authority programmes. Amongst the first targeted objectives could be petty crime in particular cities, or the amount of litter deposited on city streets, or illiteracy rates in primary schools or for adults. Local authorities could also issue Environmental Policy Bonds that target the water quality in rivers, for instance; indicators of success could be the number and variety of fish present. Unemployment amongst racial minorities, or in particular cities, could also be early targets of a Social Policy Bond regime. Such contained, easily identifiable, goals would help the bonds gain acceptability amongst the public, and encourage policymakers to discuss and refine the concept. Monitoring the behaviour of, or on behalf of, holders of such local bond issues would be a fairly simple matter. And if local authorities issued bonds in tranches, remedying any negative behaviour would also be simple. Later tranches of bonds could incorporate provisos stipulating that they would be redeemed only if the unwanted, and previously untargeted, activity did not exceed a minimal level.

Of course, bond issuing authorities would also apply lessons learned to future bond issues, while government could collate and apply these lessons before issuing bonds with national application. When bonds target certain indicators for the first time, they are especially likely to encourage unanticipated negative behaviour by bondholders. Lessons learned from such initial issues could be applied to later issues targeting the same objective. These lessons would extend beyond how to deal with bondholders' behaviour. They might, for instance, give some direction as to the circumstances under which bonds are best used as complements to existing policies, and when they can fully replace them.

A cautious, gradual, introduction of Social Policy Bonds is one means by which adjustment problems can be minimised. If, despite such an approach, bondholders behaved illegally, government could prosecute the perpetrators. If bondholders behaved in negative, but legal ways, government has other options. In ascending order of severity, government could:

- persuade or cajole bondholders into toeing the line. It could do this publicly or privately—initially, at least, bondholdings would be registered in the same way as shares.
- buy back bonds, which would have the effect of lowering the market price of bonds remaining on the market (by reducing the total redemption funds—see chapter 3, above);
- legislate against the unforeseen activity; or
- declare the bonds null and void, and offer compensation related to the bonds' issue price, or their current market price.

Effects on government's behaviour

Another possible problem arising from the integration of Social Policy Bonds into the current policy-making system arises from government's role as creator of statutes. We mentioned this above in connection with holders of bonds targeting crime, who may think it worthwhile to lobby government for longer prison sentences. Government can pass laws affecting the bond price, or its actions could influence the bond price in other ways. For instance: government could come under great pressure not to increase unemployment benefits from holders of bonds targeting unemployment. Note, though, that the source of the pressure, and the motivation for it, would be easy to identify. And lobbying is a legitimate activity. There is no reason why bondholders, in common with other pressure groups, should not lobby politicians. They would be doing so mainly out of financial self-interest of course. But other pressure groups are also self-interested, and in the case of bondholders their self-interest is, or should be, congruent with society's interests. Bondholders will lobby for legislative change, and they will benefit in obvious, financial ways. Potential investors in the bonds will take into account the likely influence of bondholders on legislation, and the potential influence of changes in legislation on the speed at which the targeted objective is achieved, when they assess the value of the bonds.

These influences make it important for there to be some element of consultation when selecting targeted objectives. People do become rich by using their influence on politicians under the current system, but they are less identifiable, and they do so in ways that are not always easy to identify. It is up to politicians to weigh the evidence for and against any course of action promoted by lobbyists, with due regard to the lobbyists' motivation. And it is up to potential investors in Social Policy Bonds to take into account likely or possible changes in the legislative environment when bidding for the bonds.

The threat of bondholders lobbying governments for legislative changes can have a positive aspect. For bond issues to be as successful as possible, governments would ideally give assurances as to their future behaviour. These could mean making relatively simple decisions early on. They might, for instance, decide now on the type of reading test to be used to determine literacy in a decade's time. But they could also extend to government's spending plans. To take bonds targeting national crime rates, for example, would-be bondholders would be very interested to know as much as they can about government's projected expenditure on the police. Similarly, prospective purchasers of bonds targeting atmospheric pollution will want to know, for instance, the government's petrol taxation, electricity generation or road building plans. Government would maximise interest in the bonds by being as open about its legislative and spending intentions as soon as possible. Government could also undertake *not* to do such things as reduce police numbers—such assurances would doubtless be subject to the usual skepticism surrounding pronouncements of this type.

Of course, if the bonds target only small changes in crime rates, or air pollution, or whatever, the government's long-range plans will not be so significant to prospective bondholders. Targeting incremental improvements in social indicators, it may emerge after trials of the bond concept, could be the best way of dealing with the uncertainties of future government behaviour. Alternatively it may be that, in many cases, such behaviour turns out to be a relatively insignificant component of the uncertainty that attaches to investment in any financial instrument: markets deal with uncertainty by attaching lower values to riskier instruments.

Government, income maintenance and eligibility criteria

While government's assurances about its future behaviour will exercise investors' minds, they will also be important to people who are consumers of government services. We shall say more on the specification of targeted objectives and indicators below, but we should note here the implications of bonds that target welfare expenditure. Examples would be bonds that, aiming to tackle unemployment, specified that they would be redeemed only when spending on unemployment benefit fell by a certain level. Bondholders would then have an incentive to discourage people from applying for, or continuing to receive, unemployment benefit. Lobbying government not to increase unemployment benefit is one thing—lobbying government to *reduce* unemployment benefit is another. While it is difficult to imagine bondholders' doing so, and thereby incurring the wrath of much of the rest of society, there are no compelling reasons for making such lobbying illegal. But where government *should* draw the line, firmly, is on the question of who decides whether or not a person qualifies for state benefits. Decisions as to eligibility for state benefits must remain with the state. This is mainly for ethical reasons: these benefits are set, ultimately, by the political process, and are anyway little more than a safety net for most recipients. Bondholders should have the right to provide alternatives to these benefits; even to pay people not to claim them. But they should not have the right to decide who should qualify for them.

The question of government behaviour can be seen in a different light. Government, as well as bondholders and society in general, would want Social Policy Bonds to be successful. Its assurances about its legislative and spending plans will never be absolute, but by giving what assurances it can a government would enhance the market for the bonds, and be able to achieve more social goals with its limited budget. One way of doing this would be to specify that future levels of unemployment benefit, state pensions, or any other benefit, will be determined by levels of objective criteria, such as price indices.

Assessment of indicators and insider trading

Government will have to organise reliable and accurate monitoring of the targeted problem so that progress towards the attainment of the social objective can be impartially assessed. This monitoring must also be seen to be independent of bondholders, who could benefit unfairly from dubious data collection. Naturally the information as to how close the objective is to being achieved will have value. It is not difficult, for instance, to imagine the latest unemployment figures being sought in advance of official publication and used for 'insider trading' purposes. If too much insider trading went on, it would increase the riskiness of the bonds to those without access to this information and so tarnish their value as an investment. How can it be minimised?

In many cases data gathering and collation would have to be more transparent. There would be a ready market for this information, which would help to make these processes more robust. There would be more interest in more frequently updated information, so that progress toward achieving objectives could be more readily charted. If large sums of money were at stake, there would be a great deal of private information gathering: investors, bondholders, and financial commentators will be taking their own soundings during the lifetime of each bond issue. All this would serve to keep the official information assessors honest.

Those involved in gathering, collating and processing information would be bound by terms deterring or forbidding them from abusing privileged information.

Indicators for targeted objectives could be chosen with view to minimising the possibility of insider trading being an important factor. Combinations of indicators could shorten the length of the information chain. The same effect could be achieved by a national government stipulating that bonds targeting such objectives as urban atmospheric pollution or crime rates in cities would be redeemed on the basis of data from a random sample of cities, rather than all cities, or a known set of cities.

The objectives themselves could be chosen to minimise the possibility of insider trading. Bonds targeting long range objectives such as cutting crime rates or unemployment by 50 percent rather than 10 percent, would probably be less sensitive to insider trading. With long range objectives, each datum illegally withheld from the bond market would probably represent a smaller proportion of the total relevant information available to the bond market, and so have a lesser effect on the bond's market value.

None of these ways of mitigating insider trading will always be fully effective. That said, there are already sensitive indicators, such as unemployment or retail sales figures, that are capable of moving markets, and so there are already in place mechanisms to keep such information secret until it is time for publication. There are also sanctions against those who obtain, and act on, such information illegally. These mechanisms and sanctions might need to be strengthened under a bond regime, but it remains to be seen how important abuse of insider information will be. While insider trading does mean that unscrupulous people benefit at the expense of the public, it does not generally impede the operation of markets. Markets continue to function and the possibility that a low level of insider trading goes on is generally discounted by the broader market.

Government as purchaser of bonds

Government agencies could, as competitive suppliers of objective-achieving services, participate as active investors in Social Policy Bonds, under certain conditions. Unlike in industry the private sector would be unlikely to cry 'unfair competition', even if the operations of these agencies were heavily subsidised, because its own bonds would appreciate as a result of the government, or government-inspired, activity.

If government agencies were to participate in the Social Policy Bond market, they should not have privileged access to information. Also, it is important that any profits they receive, or losses that they incur, as a result, should accrue to that agency. The people who work for the agency must have the same incentives as the private sector bodies to perform efficiently. This would change the character of these agencies, and would probably lead to their ultimate divorce from the public sector.

Existing institutions and the transition to a Social Policy Bond regime

Few bodies charged with achieving social goals are paid in ways that encourage better performance. Nevertheless these bodies are the main repositories of expertise for solving social problems, and some of them are bound to be efficient, or to be capable of being efficient, in doing so. It would be unwise as well as unfair and unnecessary to cut their funding too severely. The answer, at least for goals in policy areas for which there are already significant institutions, is a gradual transition.

Take health, for example. In the UK, central government provides funding for health authorities (for spending on doctors, hospitals and prescriptions) according mainly to population level, age and need. Government also directly supplies funds for research into diseases to research institutes and academic institutions. A transition to an outcome-based, rather than institution- or activity-based funding programme, would see this the funds from government gradually decline, while expenditure allocated via Social Policy Bonds to the outcomes that these institutions are collectively trying to achieve—longer life spans and a higher quality of life—would gradually rise.

The introduction of such a bond regime could see direct government funding of health authorities and research institutes fall by 1 percent a year, in real terms. (The government could allocate the saved funding to the future redemption of the health bonds it has issued.) So after five years, each health authority would be receiving directly from central government only 95 percent of what it formerly received. But holders of bonds targeting general health outcomes may choose to supplement the income of some of these health bodies. They may judge a particular group of health authorities to be especially effective at converting the funds they receive into measurable health benefits, as defined by their bonds' redemption terms. Particularly effective health authorities are likely to be working in deprived areas, where small outlays typically bring about larger improvements in health. Or bondholders may judge that a particular research body is worthy of additional funding, because it is conducting excellent research into a disease that is likely to respond especially effectively, in terms of health outcomes, to additional expenditure. In such cases, bondholders would supplement their selected health authorities' or research institutes' funding. It may well be that these favoured bodies end up receiving considerably more than 100 percent of their former income, throughout the lifetime of a bond regime.

It could also happen that investors in bonds targeting health look at completely new ways of achieving health objectives; ways that currently receive no, or very little, funding. To give a not entirely unbelievable example, they may be convinced that one of the best ways of achieving society's health objectives is to deter teenagers from driving. Following this logic, they may find that one of the most efficient ways of doing this is to provide subsidised taxis for teenagers attending parties. It is difficult to imagine how our current activity- or institution- based government fund allocation mechanisms could decide on such a programme. More generally, it is quite likely that holders of bonds targeting health outcomes would greatly expand funding in areas such as health education or preventive medicine that rely on expertise outside those bodies traditionally devoted to health care.

Could bonds targeting remote objectives, such as increasing longevity significantly, or reducing the crime rate by half, be compatible with a gradual transition of the type described above, where funding to existing health institutions reduces by 1 percent annually? At first sight there is an apparent mismatch between such incremental reductions in government spending, and the time scale needed to bring about long range objectives. The critical point here is that bondholders will be investing not on the basis of the annual reductions in government expenditure on existing health institutions, but on the basis of the redemption value of all the bonds issued. To be more precise, it will be this total redemption value, minus the bonds' existing market value, that will inform bondholders' investment decisions. This sum could be many times each year's incremental reduction in government's institution-based spending. One of the virtues of a Social Policy Bond regime is that *even in the short term bondholders would begin to invest in projects with a long range objective*, on the expectation of capital gains that may arise only in the distant future.

The accumulated reductions in spending to existing institutions would be one, but not the only, factor influencing how much government decides to spend on achieving a specified social goal. Also important would be the financial savings (if any) that achieving the objective would bring about, and the value society places on any nonfinancial benefits.

Similar, very gradual, transitions would be warranted in other areas, such as education and crime, where schools and police forces, some of which are bound to be much more effective than others, are well entrenched. These institutions would receive slowly diminishing absolute levels of funding directly from government, while bondholders would again focus their spending on especially rewarding, in terms of specified education and crime outcomes, projects and institutions. As with health, it is likely that those areas that are most disadvantaged would again provide bondholders with the greatest return per unit outlay.

In newer policy areas, particularly the environment, it may be possible to expand spending allocated via the bonds at a faster rate: expertise in the environment is still relatively mobile, and it would be easier to quickly establish new outcome-based institutions or to reorientate existing ones.

Interaction with existing programmes and projects

Note that, while changes in the source of funds would be gradual, those involved in existing institutions may well react by quickly reviewing how *all* their existing programmes and projects operate. If bondholders see existing programmes as being particularly effective in achieving targeted outcomes, then they will be inclined to invest in them. On the one hand, the switch in funding tells existing institutions that they can expect to see their relatively ineffective operations receive diminishing funds in the future. On the other hand, their effective operations can look forward to higher—possibly much higher—funding. Even a gradual transition—involving 1 percent annual cuts in funds allocated to existing institutions—that was balanced by Social Policy Bonds could bring about a rapid change in the way existing bodies conduct *all* their programmes. They may have to devote some of their resources into persuading bondholders of the cost-effectiveness of their activities; but this would not represent a radical difference from the way these bodies currently lobby for government funding nowadays. Under a bond regime, though, they would do their lobbying on a more transparent, outcome-oriented, basis.

What happens once an objective has been achieved, and the bonds redeemed?

Once an objective is close to achievement, the issuing body can float a new set of Social Policy Bonds aimed at maintaining the achieved outcome, or at further improvements. Sustaining the outcome beyond the period specified in the original bond issue is likely to be cheaper than achieving it, while further improvements targeted by a second bond issue are likely to cost less, in terms of benefit per unit outlay, than those achieved by the first issue. There are three main reasons for this, the first two of which are linked:

Assume that a bond issue that boosted some targeted indicator from a level of 70 to 80 in one year had a net cost of one million dollars. In many cases it would take more than a withdrawal of this funding for the indicator to revert back to 70. Why? If the indicator represents the rate, in percent, of unemployment in one area, for example, many of the newly employed would stay in work, even if the absence of expenditure on a bond issue meant that their salary would revert to the level that had previously failed to attract them into work. This would be partly because they are now more aware of the existence of low-paid work, partly because of the costs and disruption of reverting to an unemployed lifestyle and partly because they now find the prospect of being unemployed less attractive than previously. If the indicator represented the cleanliness of air, to take another example, maintaining lower levels of pollution could be cheaper than achieving it because people have invested in machinery or other systems that cost less, per unit benefit, to keep running than they did to set up.

In a similar fashion, investors in Social Policy Bonds would learn from their experience of achieving the objective targeted by the first bond issue. They would have looked for, and experimented with, different methods of solving the targeted social problem, and be able to choose the most efficient ones for subsequent bond issues. If maintaining the cleanliness of a river, for instance, were targeted, then it is likely that any know-how about monitoring systems or equipment installation would be more cheaply available once an initial targeted lower level had already been achieved.

Less specifically, it is likely that general improvements in productivity, mainly arising from technology (including information technology), will continue to occur in our economies, and that bondholders will make use of them.

Conclusion

The introduction of a Social Policy Bond regime will be accompanied by operational challenges and problems, not all of which will be anticipated. But these potential problems should not be overstated. Existing laws, careful choice and specification of targeted objectives, more transparency in government as to what it wants to achieve and how it will behave will probably circumvent or remedy most of them. And many of the problems that a bond regime would entail are the inevitable result of policies that have as their measure of achievement quantifiable indicators. Regardless of Social Policy Bonds, the trend toward using more of these indicators is likely to continue; and they will always be contentious. Consider the controversy that swirls around school league tables, for example, or suggested indicators of climate change.

The point is that the question of how well Social Policy Bonds would achieve society's goals needs to be considered alongside current policy-making methods. In today's political environment policymakers, officials, or lobbyists, can escape or deflect censure because the adverse results of their policies are difficult to relate to their cause. If Social Policy Bonds were to lead to negative effects, the relationship between these effects and their cause would be more easy to identify, and deterring such effects would be more simple, than doing so under the current activity—or institutional- based funding arrangements.

Chapter 5

Advantages of a Social Policy Bond regime over the current system

Efficiency

The main advantage of Social Policy Bonds is that, because they would inject self-interest into all stages necessary for solving social problems, they would be *more cost-effective* than current, activity-based programmes. For the same government expenditure, therefore, more can be achieved.

I have discussed above the fact that the bonds would give people an incentive to carry out existing activities efficiently. But as important is the fact that the bonds would encourage people to

- investigate new activities; and
- experiment with different activities in different regions.

One of the problems with government supplying social services is that it has real difficulty investigating new approaches. This is partly because government, historically, has always been more interested in preventing failure than in rewarding success. It cannot afford to try new approaches, for fear that if they fail it will be branded as irresponsible. It cannot readily try different ideas in different regions, because then it would have to face criticism from people who had experienced the less successful ideas. And because the government's income is compulsorily levied on taxpayers, on pain of imprisonment, it feels it should carry out only those activities that it can plausibly justify on the basis of a past record. These need not be very efficient, or even partly efficient. As far as the government is concerned, they need only to have been tried in the past, and not to have been widely identified as disastrous. This is not a strategy designed to optimise performance; rather it is a strategy that minimises the perceived risk of failure. It leads to the continuing of inefficient, unimaginative activities, whose main recommendation is that they have been well-tried. As the persistence of social problems attests, these have not been very successful.

In some policy areas, such as education, or the environment, it is all too easy for government to override the wishes of individual schools or private property owners, because it thinks it knows best. Where government has the power, it often adopts a single approach, which it follows until the deficiencies of doing so become impossible to ignore. Individual schools, or private property owners, on the other hand, employ diverse approaches and adjust them as the situation requires. The conceit that government knows best was never exclusive to the Communist countries. The fact is that all the alternative solutions for many social and environmental problems are *not* known in advance, and that the optimal choice is seldom a one-size fits all, top-down, government-dictated policy. More often, it is a matter for investigation and experimentation, and a wide variety of approaches is essential.

Under a Social Policy Bond regime, each of any diverse activities would be rewarded in direct proportion to their success. And once applied they, or an optimal combination of them, would become the new standard for future projects.

The same reasoning applies to the undertaking of different activities in different regions, or more generally, to different local conditions. In one area, for example, crime may be a very direct result of unemployment. But under the current crime-reduction regime there is very little incentive for anyone to explore this link, and see whether diverting funds from, say, the police to employment creation on a small scale, would be a better way of fighting crime. For example, a factory closure might be expected to lead to a soaring crime rate in one particular locality where, perhaps, young males would be put out of work. But government would find it politically difficult to subsidise the continued operation of just that one factory, when similar factories around the country are just as uneconomic, but the people working in them are less likely to commit crimes if their factories close. Another hypothetical example: screening for certain forms of cancer might be found to be of particular benefit only to women in poorer households. Yet the government would find it politically very difficult to deny such screening to *all* women. In a Social Policy Bond regime, bondholders would put maximisation of their return per unit outlay, which is *also maximisation of the returns from cancer-screening to the taxpayer's pound*, above such considerations.

So government is often constrained from trying different approaches, not just because it is inefficient generally but because, when it does respond, it has to *appear* to be responsible and even-handed. This often goes hand-in-hand with government's tendency to enlarge its own role. Compliance costs of coping with burdensome regulations in areas such as schools and small businesses are one example. Here, for instance, potential employers are deterred from starting a business, because government insists that would-be employees are at risk from, for example, an absence of fire escapes. Government denies people the choice of whether to accept a slightly higher risk of a fatal accident at work, in return for a job. While it is all very well to protect workers in this way, when people cannot find work locally they have to travel. In doing so they may well face a risk of dying in a car accident far higher than that of being trapped in a building with no fire escapes.

Government often applies its regulations regardless of whether they are appropriate in particular circumstances. Of many examples of regulation that could be cited as inappropriate, to the point of absurdity, my own favourite is this: the European Union insists that abattoirs be tiled. Logic therefore dictated that a snail farmer was told to tile his packing room, which was classed as an abattoir, up to the ceiling to catch the blood.[18]

Social Policy Bonds would encourage investigation of local circumstances, on the basis that it could lead to more efficient solution of the social problem affecting a much larger region, or the whole country. In similar fashion they would stimulate diverse responses to a particular problem. Bondholders might find, after a bit of experimenting with different approaches, that certain activities work better than others under certain conditions. They would take the best of these approaches, and apply them where their return would be greatest, and they would recognise that, for certain objectives, a mosaic of diverse activities is most efficient.

Transparency

Social Policy Bonds also make policy objectives more *transparent*. By focusing on outcomes, rather than activities, social objectives are explicitly identified, while indirect, as well as

---

18. *Country File*, BBC1 channel, BBC television, UK, 8 February 1998.

direct, means of achieving them are encouraged—but only if bondholders think them more efficient. Focusing on identifiable outcomes would encourage constructive participation in the political process, and means that measures taken to achieve them would be more likely to attract public support. At least as important, all outcomes would have to be *costed*. This means that the maximum value that society wishes to place on an outcome will have to be decided and publicly known before any programmes have begun. Once that has been determined, the issuing body will be able to decide on the bonds' redemption value and the number of bonds to be issued. Costing outcomes in this way would make the tradeoffs between social outcomes more transparent, and make more realistic people's expectations of government. In today's politics, costs of achieving outcomes are obscure, and the language of political debate, at least in the mass media, rarely includes the crucial concept of tradeoffs between different social goals.

Transparency in goal-setting would make virtually impossible two further obstacles on the way to efficient achievement of social goals:

- **'Capture' by bureaucrats:** transparency over policy goals would mean that government would be unlikely to name itself the beneficiary of its own policies. So it would mean the decoupling of governments' advisory functions from the service delivery functions that it carries out today.
- **Taxpayers' funding of middle class welfare:** the bonds would make explicit the desired outcomes, and so would make it very difficult for projects whose result has been to tax the poor for the benefit of the middle class or the rich, to be launched.

Transparency means clear and explicit objectives. To give one example, the Common Agricultural Policy, with its vague and mutually conflicting objectives, would never have made it over this first hurdle of rational policymaking. Social Policy Bonds would force a rethink on other policy issues. Drugs policy, for instance. Under a Social Policy Bond regime hard questions would need to be asked. Is a reduction in drug taking an end in itself, or a means to an end? If the latter, then what are these ends, and wouldn't we be better off targeting them directly? Unemployment may also have to be seen in a new light. Again, is lower unemployment an end in itself? Or a means to an end? Some studies have indeed suggested that the strongest influence on happiness is employment: people with jobs are very much happier than the unemployed.[19] But if lower unemployment is seen as a way of ensuring that fewer people fall below a certain income level; or if it is seen as a means towards a lower crime rate, or better mental health of the population, then some combination of these objectives should be the targets for government policy. Answers to questions such as these would be unavoidable *at the outset* of a Social Policy Bond issue, but they are rarely posed, and still more rarely answered, under the existing policymaking regime. So current government programmes bumble along with no clear objectives, and as a result are wasteful or even counterproductive.

In fact, even under the existing regime there is increased pressure for accountability within government. The trend is for taxpayers to ask more and more questions about what government programmes are actually for, especially as efforts to rein in public spending have so obviously failed. Transparent social goals require a transparent process for formulating them. A

---

19. see, for example, 'Happiness is a warm vote', the Economist, 17 April 1999.

Ronnie Horesh

Social Policy Bond regime would use answers to these questions not as ammunition in a bigger- or smaller- government debate, but as a way of developing effective policy tools, to achieve what society actually wants to achieve.

A clear expression of desired social outcomes would also mean that progress toward them could be accurately monitored. Perhaps that is one reason why it has rarely been a major feature of government activity over the decades.

Stability

The bonds also guarantee *stability* of policy objectives. Social Policy Bonds could target goals with a necessarily long lead time and bondholders would not be deterred from taking measures to achieve them by fears of a reversal of government policy—or, indeed, a change of government. Only the ends, not the means, would be laid down by government. Obviously the objectives will have to be carefully defined, but there is a wide consensus over what constitutes most social goals. A government is unlikely to repudiate such universally desired *objectives*, even if the associated Social Policy Bonds had been issued by a ruling party with a different political outlook. The risk that it might (and so become the first government *openly* to support higher unemployment, lower standards of health care, etc) would be not much greater than that of a government refusing to redeem fixed interest stock issued by any of its predecessors. This risk, always present, is factored into bond prices, and in no way impedes the operation of bond markets.

Importantly, for the bonds to be as successful as possible, governments would have to give assurances as to their future behaviour. For maximum success, they would also have to choose

– 65 –

their objectives in consultation with opposition political parties, as well as with the electorate.

Because Social Policy Bonds can target broad objectives, which are more likely to be stable over time, they have *informational advantages* over policies that have narrow objectives. As an example, let us take the myriad ways in with health care funding can be allocated. The government has to make these resource allocation decisions on the basis of data that are necessarily incomplete. How can the government know in detail the effect that spending on, say, cancer diagnostic machinery will have on the overall health of the nation, as compared with subsidising the cost of nicotine chewing gum? So, by default, health expenditure is influenced by groups of medical specialists with little incentive or capacity to see improvements in the *general* health of the nation as an objective. As a result, funding of these specialities depends to a great *and varying* extent, on the strength of their lobby groups, rather than on accurate scientific information. So what is arguably the most efficient way of spending the taxpayer's health pound – preventive medicine – receives derisory funding because it has no powerful lobbyists.

Stable objectives also mean that rational allocation of resources will not be undermined by high-profile events. As I write this, the British Government is coming under considerable pressure to order the installation of an automatic breaking system for trains that go through red signals, in the aftermath of a tragic rail disaster in London that resulted in the death of more around 40 people. Cold calculations show that this would cost around £14 million for each life that the system would be expected to save. This is around five times the figure that the British Treasury uses as its benchmark—which means that many more lives could be saved if this money were to be spent saving lives in other ways. That would be a seemingly heartless decision to make, in the circumstances—

but it would be the right one, and under a Social Policy Bond regime there is no question that it would be taken.

Stability of objectives, as opposed to activities, also means that uncertain scientific relationships need not be proven before work can begin on achieving desired outcomes. Take, for example, climate change.

Climate change, the Kyoto Agreement and Environmental Policy Bonds[20]

The evidence that the global climate is changing is large and growing. That said, scientists are divided as to whether (a) how fast climate is changing, (b) the effects of climate change, (c) how much man should do about it, and (d) whether how much man *can* do about it. it is undesirable, or how undesirable it is, if it is happening.

There is enough evidence, though, to convince many scientists that climate change is happening, that it would be a bad thing, and that we can at least slow the pace of climate change by limiting emissions of greenhouse gases. Even if we are uncertain, climate change has the potential to inflict serious harm on many people, so there is a strong argument for doing what we can to make sure it doesn't happen. The December 1997 Kyoto agreement ('Kyoto') saw 159 nations reach the world's first legally binding commitments to reduce the global output of carbon dioxide and five other gases thought to contribute to the 'greenhouse' effect. Thirty-eight industrialised countries agreed

---

20. Note; in this book I use 'Environmental Policy Bonds' to mean bonds targeting exclusively environmental objectives. But the term 'Social Policy Bonds' can be taken to include Environmental Policy Bonds in most contexts. The principle is the same.

to reduce emissions by 2012 to an average of 5.2 per cent below what they were in 1990. The US target, for example, requires a 7 per cent reduction below 1990 levels, which essentially would mean cutting emissions by up to 40 per cent compared to what they would otherwise have been 14 years from now. The agreement provides for an emissions-trading scheme and other market-based mechanisms to making it easier to comply, but it would not force developing countries to accept binding limits on their emissions in the near future.

The Kyoto targets are far lower than what some environmentalists had hoped for, and what some countries, most notably the European Union, had been advocating. It was clear to the Kyoto negotiators that the treaty would only slow, but not stop, the buildup of carbon dioxide and other greenhouse gases in the atmosphere. (Carbon dioxide, which is given off by fossil fuel combustion, is thought to be by far the most important of the man-made greenhouse gases that form an insulating blanket around Earth.) But subsequent evaluations by leading scientists indicate that the environmental effects may be so small as to be almost unnoticeable in the near term.

In an analysis published in the journal *Science*[21] (January 1998), Bert Bolin, a Swedish meteorologist and the outgoing chairman of the United Nations Intergovernmental Panel on Climate Change, predicted that levels of carbon dioxide in the atmosphere will climb to 382 parts per million by 2010 if countries comply with their Kyoto commitments. That would represent an increase of 8 per cent from 1990 levels, but a decline of only 0.4 per cent from the level it would have been had no

---

21. quoted in 'Reassessing Kyoto Agreement: Scientists See Little Environmental Advantage', Joby Warrick, *the Washington Post* 13 February 1998.

actions were taken. Other scientists have estimated that the Kyoto agreement would slow the projected rise in global temperatures by one-tenth to two-tenths of one degree Celsius by 2050.

Such a reduction would be 'an important first step' but would be 'far from what is required to reach the goal of stabilizing the concentration of in the atmosphere,' wrote Bolin.

Other climate experts agree with the essence of Bolin's conclusions, if not with all the specifics. But some fear that governments will cite the modest environmental benefits as an excuse for doing nothing. Even if all industrialized countries honour their commitments to reduce pollution, levels of heat-trapping greenhouse gases in the atmosphere will continue to grow.

Concentration of carbon dioxide in the atmosphere (parts per million)

Assuming full compliance with Kyoto treaty

1990: 353
2010: 382   With no reductions in emissions 2010: 383.5

Source: Bert Bolin, Intergovernmental Panel on Climate Change

------

More technical weaknesses are that Kyoto: is largely silent on how to calculate or verify credits for human-induced sink activities; and that it makes no provision for credits for the buildup of a country's agricultural soil carbon sink.

So the Kyoto agreement, in summary, is an agreement that was certainly divisive and is likely to have little chance of success in achieving even a significant reduction in greenhouse gases. It will certainly be expensive to administer, and will impose large costs on the world's economies. All these costs, political and financial, might well be worthwhile, if Kyoto is successful in stabilising the world's climate. The real problem is that there is no guarantee that it will do so.

If climate change is not actually happening as quickly as currently thought, or is not going to be significantly affected by Kyoto's envisaged reduction in greenhouse gas emissions, then Kyoto will be an expensive failure. Yet climate change could unleash unimaginable disasters on many parts of the globe. It would be irresponsible to do nothing until the vast majority of scientists agree that there is a problem. Is there a better solution?

Environmental Policy Bonds deal with this uncertainty quite neatly. Environmental Policy Bonds would bypass the means, and focus directly on the end that society wants to achieve: a more stable world climate. (Many say that climate change—as distinct from climate variability—will actually be a good thing—leading to longer growing seasons and higher yields, while others forecast drought, disease and violent storms. Others point to the boost to crop productivity given by higher levels of atmospheric carbon dioxide.[22]) There are difficulties involved in defining what a stable climate actually is, *but the same difficulties apply when attempting to monitor the success or otherwise of the Kyoto agreement, or other such initiatives targeting greenhouse gas emissions,* where the relationship between what is targeted and what is required is unknown. How are we to know whether these expensive cuts in emissions are taking us closer to our objective of a more stable global climate? Presumably scientists will measure

---

22. See, for example, *The great promise of the 'Greenhouse Effect'*, Sylvan H Wittwer, Consumers Research, June 1997.

the effects of the Kyoto Agreement by recording such objectively verifiable indicators, as temperature, change in temperature, rate of change of temperature, frequency and severity of extreme weather events, precipitation, and so on.

So why not target a combination of these indicators directly? That is what Environmental Policy Bonds targeting climate change would do. Governments would issue these bonds, which would be redeemable *only when the climate had achieved an agreed level of stability.* Once issued, these bonds would stimulate cost-effective and unbiassed research into the causes of climate change. But they will not make assumptions as to *how* to stabilise the world's climate—that is left to bondholders.

It may well be that greenhouse gas emissions are responsible for climate change. But it may also be that other factors are even more crucial. Scientific knowledge about climate change is uncertain, and improving continuously. Environmental Policy Bonds targeting climate change directly may well lead to cuts in greenhouse gas emissions if these are found to be the most cost-effective solution, but they would not prejudge the scientific relationships involved. Policies like Kyoto responding to effects whose causes are uncertain, embody fixed ideas about the nature of the relationships involved. As scientific knowledge improves therefore, the flaws in such policies are likely to become increasingly obvious.

Internationally-backed bonds targeting climate stability would be issued by a world body, perhaps one set up by the United Nations, perhaps using funds paid by all countries, in proportion to their Gross National Products. It would be up to individual countries to decide how to raise funds, presumably from taxation revenue.

As with other Social Policy Bonds, bondholders will choose a range of projects in which to invest. They could:

- help finance companies' or countries' greenhouse gas emission control programmes;
- subsidise, or pay for, companies or countries' carbon sequestration plantations;
- subsidise production or consumption of energy that involves lower greenhouse gas emissions;
- attempt to stabilise the global climate by increasing the planet's albedo;
- carry out, or subsidise, research into the causes of climate change.

Bondholders would undertake whichever climate-stabilising projects give them the best return for their outlay. That could entail tackling the causes of climate change, whether manmade or natural. Or it could mean looking for, and using, new technology to attenuate climate variability.

Apart from the usual advantages of a Social Policy Bond regime, climate stability bonds represent a big improvement over Kyoto in that it makes no assumptions based on existing scientific knowledge. There may be other manmade or natural effects on climate stability that are far more important, but of which we are currently unaware. It is certainly true that natural variability of climate has had severe impacts on human life in the past.[23] Kyoto, responding to effects whose causes are uncertain, embodies a limited number of fixed ideas about the nature of the relationships

---

23. See, for example, the references cited by Overpeck, J. T. Nature **403**, 714-715 (2000).

involved. A CSB regime, targeting climate change directly, may well lead to cuts in greenhouse gas emissions, but it would not assume that doing so is the best solution. CSBs improve on Kyoto, because they encourage behaviour leading to the desired outcome, rather than seeking to control activities whose effects on the climate stability are not fully understood.

Similar considerations apply in other policy areas, where scientific relationships are unproven, or unstable over time. Take health: targeting broad indicators of well-being – life expectancy, infant mortality, disability – would ensure that scarce resources are allocated in ways that would directly achieve *society's* health objectives. It would be up to bondholders to explore the scientific and financial relationships so as to divert, impartially, their funding into those existing or new areas of the health service that would most efficiently use them to achieve the targeted broad outcomes.

More generally, most social and environmental problems will require a range of different projects for their solution. The way these projects affect each other, and their effects on the ultimate social objective will not be known in advance, and will vary with time and circumstances. Social Policy Bonds have stable objectives, but they will always be encouraging the range of approaches that is thought to be most efficient with the knowledge available at any the time. This occurs because of the nature of the bond mechanism, and requires no advance selection by government of the most efficient combination of programmes. Only the objective, not the ways of achieving it, would be decided by government.

More attractive money flows

A further advantage of Social Policy Bonds is that, in many cases, they will have *more politically appealing money flows*. As an example, consider the environment. Some current methods of pollution control inflict identifiable losses on certain people in pursuit of vague objectives. Social Policy Bonds, however, would reward people for achieving successful outcomes. The Bonds would of course be redeemed by funds from the government's general taxation revenue and taxes would still have to be levied to provide this, but there is, nevertheless, a presentational advantage.

The other, more significant, money flow advantage of Social Policy Bonds is that the government would incur expenditure only when definite outcomes had actually been achieved. For this reason, the bonds may attract greater political support for certain causes than agency- or activity- based programmes.

Correlation with public benefit

A less obvious distributional benefit of a Social Policy Bond regime would arise from the existence of a means of acquiring wealth whereby private gain is strongly and inextricably correlated with public benefit. Many bondholders, whether institutions or individuals, would start out rich and, if their bonds were redeemed, would become richer. But working to achieve desired social goals would be seen to be a socially acceptable way of acquiring wealth. There are intangible benefits from having people or institutions grow rich in this way. There are many disaffected people for whom the perceived social benefits of the activities performed by today's large corporations are difficult to square with their (apparently) very large profits. They are also unconvinced that 'trickle-down' occurs to any meaningful degree. Wealth, in these people's eyes, is the result of exploitation. Social Policy Bonds would help such people take a more positive view of earning an income and accumulating wealth, and could make for a more cohesive society.

I hesitate to mention also the fact that the existence of a means by which private gain is so inextricably tied to social benefit could make more acceptable the taxing of other, less edifying, means of acquiring wealth—inheritance, for example. I hesitate, because I believe a Social Policy Bond regime would lead to a general and significant *lowering* of the tax bill, which could make tax increases unnecessary.

Chapter 6

Comparison with other 'more-market' approaches

Many countries' governments have recognised the inadequacies of the conventional approach to solving social problems. Recognising that the market is a far better allocator of resources than government, they have made various efforts to give the market more influence over these decisions. This chapter looks at some of these alternatives, and contrasts them with Social Policy Bonds.

Contractual approach: New Zealand state sector reform

From 1988 over a period of a few years New Zealand's public sector was radically and innovatively reformed. Tightly held central control gave way to autonomous departments, headed by chief executives with the authority to take decisions relating to the whole of their organisations. Chief executives are expected to hire and fire staff, negotiate pay, manage their finances and capital assets, negotiate purchase agreements and be held to account for outputs. Other major changes, relevant to discussion of Social Policy Bonds include:

- accountability for resources and results is maintained through contestible, contract-like arrangements within government;

- performance agreements between ministers and chief executives lay down standards and expectations for department heads; and
- purchase agreements between ministers and departments specify the outputs to be produced during the year.

The arrangements between Ministers and departments specify *ex ante* the outputs they are required to deliver, but leave Chief Executives free to select the mix of inputs to be used in producing these outputs. This system has been extended to encompass the specification of, and accountability for, longer term objectives. Since 1994 the New Zealand Government has defined the medium-term outcomes it is trying to achieve in nine 'strategic result areas' (SRAs) and linked the outputs delivered by each department to these SRAs through 'key result areas', which now form the basis for their performance agreements.

What have the results been? According to Allen Schick, in a report on the New Zealand reforms commissioned by the New Zealand Government, there been efficiency gains. However, the transactions costs incurred in negotiating agreements, monitoring compliance and preparing reports have been high, and in some cases have 'soaked up a substantial part of the efficiency gains' made from restructuring.[24]

In the context of bureaucratic change the New Zealand reforms were radical. But, in my view, they are not radical enough, and the reforms have been constrained by their institutional structure. Government departments were originally envisaged as achieving specific outcomes; but that did not

---

24. Allen Schick, *The spirit of reform: managing the New Zealand state sector in a time of change*, State Services Commission, Wellington, 1996.

occur. Instead, outputs are the measure by which departments' performance is judged, the rationale being that the supply of outputs can be directly attributed to departments' performance, while outcomes may be influenced by factors beyond their control. As Schick puts it: 'outcomes are externalities in two-party relationships; therefore it is exceedingly difficult to assign responsibility for them.' Indeed. Assigning responsibility has a high priority only because the players—those charged with doing things—are largely known in advance. The New Zealand reforms have, in effect, subordinated results to this perceived need to assign responsibility, which in turn, seems to be driven by existing institutional structures and relationships.

Tradeable permits to pollute

Tradable permits are most relevant to unpriced resources, such as the assimilative capacity of the environment. They are most widely used in pollution control, where they are most relevant for pollutants that have marked thresholds. A tradeable permit regime determines the maximum amount of pollutant that can be discharged. People then trade permits to emit amounts of pollutant making up this total. In the US, markets for permits to emit sulphur dioxide have been in operation for several years. Markets decide the price and allocation of these permits.

As we saw above ('Stability') Social Policy Bonds have informational advantages when targeting broad objectives. These advantages can apply in pollution control. Water pollution, for example, results from many sources and many different processes. Immense quantities of information would be needed to establish, monitor and enforce a comprehensive system of pollution control using tradeable permits to pollute. An Environmental Policy Bond regime, however, would simply target aggregate pollution levels, and let bondholders decide how best to achieve them.

However, tradeable permits can work well with intrinsically large-scale processes, or for controlling emissions that have no polluting substitutes. Such processes and substances can be monitored quite easily, because there would be no fear that doing so would lead to offsetting increases in pollution via the setting up of difficult-to-monitor small-scale processes, or the emission of polluting substitutes that are not being monitored. But technological and ecological complexity mean that these processes and substances are a minority. Tradeable permits to pollute can therefore play only a small role in environmental protection.

Contracting out of existing services and the UK's Private Finance Initiative

In Chapter 3, while discussing the tradeability of Social Policy Bonds, we looked at some of the limitations involved in handing responsibility for services to private contractors. When compared to Social Policy Bonds, contracting out has other disadvantages. The aim of the UK Government's Private Finance Initiative (PFI) is to encourage the private sector to invest in major public infrastructure projects, such as hospitals, schools, and roads. Under the PFI, building projects that would previously have relied on public money are financed by the private sector, instead of being paid for directly from public funds.

Taking hospitals, for example, the private sector partner is usually responsible for:

- designing the facilities, according to National Health Service (NHS) specifications;
- building the facilities, to time and at a fixed cost;

- financing the capital cost: the private sector partner recovers this cost by renting the facilities to the NHS, generally for periods of more than 25 years; and
- operating the facilities: most of the staff—certainly the cleaners, catering, porters, security and maintenance staff—are employed by the private contractor. Receptions, secretaries and lab technicians may also be employed by the private sector, but doctors and nurses are employed by the NHS.

It is the private PFI partner who assumes the risks in each of these areas; this reduces the overall risks to the public sector associated with procuring new assets. Moreover, because the PFI partner's capital is at risk, it will have a big incentive to continue to perform efficiently throughout the life of the contract.

Under the PFI, government specifies the outputs it requires, in terms of the nature and level of the service required, and invites the private sector to bid for the contract to supply these outputs. Government has, in effect, contracted out the building of the hospital, and non-health staffing, to the private sector.

The PFI, as with contracting out of services generally, is efficient at supplying carefully specified outputs. And as with the New Zealand state sector reforms specification of these outputs can be a costly exercise (though costs will fall as different public sector bodies share their output-specification experiences), as will be monitoring of compliance. But it is also quite a limited exercise, in comparison to a Social Policy Bond regime. Simply put, outputs, however efficiently supplied, do not necessarily lead to more favourable, or more efficiently supplied, outcomes. It is true that allowing the private sector to bid to supply outputs is generally more efficient than paying directly from public funds. (A report commissioned by the UK Treasury puts the average estimated saving for a sample of projects as 17 percent.[25]) But because they are only outputs, and because of the degree to which they must be specified to ensure efficiency, the contracting out of services tends:

- to be limited to particular stages of an outcome delivering enterprise; and
- to reinforce established ways of doing things.

So a new hospital may be built on time, to exact specification, and cost-effectively. But a Social Policy Bond targeting general health indicators would not assume that a new hospital was the best way of achieving society's health goals in the first place.

Contracting out has other disadvantages. Take the important example of the recent dramatic overhaul of the US welfare system. In August 1996 President Clinton signed legislation allowing states more flexible rules in the use of private contractors. States are given a lump sum to spend as they wish. Several firms have won contracts to find work for welfare recipients. Under these schemes firms can, for example, canvas local businesses for job placements. The firms receive a payment when one of their welfare recipient clients is placed; they receive a higher payment if the work is full-time after a probationary period, and another payment if they stay on beyond this period.

For the states, this means that the private sector takes the risk. They pay the private contractors only when clients are found jobs. If the contractors fail to do this, the state is no worse off. Unfortunately though, contractors have no real incentive to look after the least employable welfare claimants: the cost of finding

---

25. *Value for money drivers in the Private Finance Initiative*, Arthur Andersen and Enterprise LSE, commissioned by (UK) Treasury Taskforce, 17 January 2000.

work for the least employable claimants would far exceed the placement fee. For example, in December 1998, the US Department of Agriculture rejected a request by the state of Arizona for a waiver to allow a private company to determine eligibility for food stamps in a pilot project. Arizona wanted to allow people seeking benefits under its welfare-to-work programme to be able to apply for an array of programmes in a single visit. The Arizona state government would have given private vendors financial incentives for getting people off food stamps, and such incentives are why federal officials want states to keep using public employees to determine benefit eligibility. Federal officials also rejected a similar request from Texas.

Tradeable contracts

What if contracts were made tradeable, so that the winner of a tendered contract could sell the right to supply the service? Perhaps the successful bidding company has done what it can to achieve a targeted objective, and has done it efficiently and quickly. Then the value of the contract rises, and being tradeable, can be sold at a profit. The new contractor has as much incentive as the original to perform efficiently.

Such tradeable contracts would be similar to Social Policy Bonds, as long as the terms of the contract stipulated not that a certain output be supplied, but that a specified outcome be achieved. There would be some small differences though. Ownership of Social Policy Bonds would be more fluid, which means more market liquidity, more transparency and an enhanced ability for the government to fine tune its priorities after the outcome has been specified and the bonds issued.

Voucher schemes

Education voucher schemes have been used by several states in the north-eastern US. People are given vouchers which they can use to purchase schooling for their children, from whichever schools they want—government or private.

Vouchers would give greater importance to what people want from education, rather than what government employees or others think they should want. Most parents agree on the importance of basic academic subjects. People expect that, at a minimum, their children will have mastered reading, writing, and elementary maths by the time they are out primary school. Parents are also concerned about career preparation. But beyond these basics priorities differ widely. Vouchers allow parents to make their own decisions, and encourages schools to compete to supply what parents want.

Voucher schemes have some of the advantages of Social Policy Bonds: through markets parents are motivated to seek the best education available at the price, and schools are motivated to supply it. Under a voucher scheme government continues to pay for education. But vouchers do have some disadvantages, stemming from the fact that the vouchers don't specify outcomes. They specify only that must be used to pay for children's' going to school. This works well for those parents who are capable of making informed choices, and who are willing to do so. It does not work so well for the children of less informed or less motivated parents, and these are precisely those who most need help. So under a voucher system, it will still be possible for desired social outcomes, such as near-universal literacy, say, not to be achieved.

The problem of lack of information points to the difficulty of extending voucher schemes to areas other than education, such as health care, where similar efforts to give people purchasing power may also founder.

There are other social goals for which voucher schemes cannot work effectively: these goals have a public good element that is stronger than the private. Examples are: reduced crime rates, better environmental protection, and lower unemployment. Giving people vouchers to spend on public goods like these cannot work.

Privatisation

Privatisation is the selling of ownership of the assets owned by government suppliers of services, and the transfer of control to shareholders. It has been widespread. In many countries utilities, such as railways, electricity companies and telecoms, have been fully privatised. In the UK, most of the local authorities' housing stock has been sold to ex-tenants.

How successful has privatisation been? In those countries with rule of law and secure property rights it has been a success, at least when we look at the performance of privatised companies. They are much more profitable than previously; they are more competitive and innovative and in general they provide much better service to consumers than before they were privatised. Because of the taxes they pay on their profits, they make positive contributions to government funds—a dramatic change from when they were publicly owned and were mostly a drain on public funds. But what about the bigger picture though?

Privatisation, in the view of Dr Jonathan Michie, Lecturer at the Judge Institute of Management Studies, and a Fellow of Robinson College, Cambridge 'has created a need for very detailed public regulation of privatised industries. This has been quite at odds with what was expected by the government and its advisors.'[26] What we have now, he says, 'is not a clear

---

26. Speaking at a seminar on the 'Elusive Concept of Sovereignty', held at the Finnish Institute in April 1996.

case of the state withdrawing as an economic agent but rather changing its role as such.' Perhaps this is one reason why the overall tax burden, as we saw in Chapter 1, has continued to rise in the industrialised countries.

Privatisation of other services, such as basic education, health care, and social insurance, would probably not be politically acceptable in many areas—at least, not without further extensive regulation. The political problem is that private businesses have private goals, and while these may coincide with social goals most of the time, there will always be some who either through their own, or their parents', misfortune, indolence or apathy, will not be well-served by private institutions. This, of course, is true of the current system, but the current system can claim that because it is not private it has the public interest at heart. (It may be failing to look after the public interest, and it may be very expensive and inefficient, but it can make that claim.) A fully privatised school system, for instance, would have no market incentive to raise the educational standards of the less bright children of poor parents.

Summary: Social Policy Bonds compared with other 'more market' approaches

Both the contractual arrangements between government ministers and government agencies seen in the New Zealand state sector reforms, and the contracting out of existing services, suffer because of the need for government to specify in detail what is required. This limits their application considerably. Similarly, the information demands of tradeable pollution permits means that they can be used only for inherently large-scale processes, which can be monitored quite easily.

Noteworthy, though, from our brief look at some of the US states' contracting out job placement, is the private sector's willingness to bear the risks of finding work for the jobless. Under the UK's Private Finance Initiative, as well, it is the private sector that bears the risk of overruns on such things as construction cost. Indeed, this transfer of risk to the private sector is estimated to account for 60 percent of the forecast savings that result from the PFI.[27] The private sector's willingness to bear risk, and the savings that result, bode well for a Social Policy Bond regime, under which investors in the bonds bear all the risks of achieving outcomes. Because the bonds' prices are determined by the market, the cost of assuming all risks is fair to both the holder and the taxpayer.

But because of the limitations of the contracting out of services, it would seem that privatisation and vouchers are the most widely applicable of the 'more market' alternatives to government. A combination of privatised schools, for example, and vouchers, could do much to raise standards in education with unchanged, or even reduced, public expenditure. But note the problem of children whose parents have no ability to make an informed decision as to the schooling, or who have no interest in doing so. For education, this could turn out to be a minor problem, as the standards of all schools are likely to rise in a privatised system. But lack of information would marked in health care, where most consumers have little idea as to the treatment they need. They rely on the medical profession to tell them.

In general, when a system allows private interests to flourish, there will be some people who suffer either because they are poor, or because they are uninformed consumers. Giving the poor purchasing power would help them, so long as they can make an

---

27. Value for money drivers in the Private Finance Initiative, Arthur Andersen and Enterprise LSE, commissioned by (UK) Treasury Taskforce, 17 January 2000.

informed decision, and are willing to do so. When the service is one like education, most people will fall into that category. But when the service is one like health care, where most consumers are in the dark, the number of uninformed, or misinformed, people will be very large.

Social Policy Bonds would solve this information problem in ways that privatisation plus vouchers cannot. They would give a voice to, and focus directly on, *society's* concerns. Compared to a privatisation plus vouchers regime, they would:

- have some advantages in education where some people's children may fall through the cracks;
- have significant advantages health care, where most people are uninformed, and there are important public good aspects in having a healthy population; and
- have major advantages in areas like crime and the environment, where again the public good aspects are important, and where there is no pricing mechanism for consumers to make their choices known.

For the same reasons, they also have political advantages. Most of the arguments in favour of continued government intervention in areas like health, education, and welfare crystalise around what would happen to the poor if government were to withdraw. Social Policy Bonds are, I believe, superior to other 'more market' approaches, in that government does not relinquish its role in bringing about better outcomes for the poorest members of society. It simply withdraws from *achieving* these goals, but continues to define these goals, and to be the ultimate source of finance for their achievement. The political reality is that there *is* such a thing as society, and society's goals may be different from an aggregation of all its members' individual goals, weighted by purchasing power. As a society, there are things like lower infant mortality, or

100 per cent literacy, which we may want to achieve, and know we can achieve, but which a fully privatised system will not guarantee. Social Policy Bonds, because they are outcome-oriented, allow full discussion and consultation as to what society's goals are, and how much society values their achievement. They then encourage people to go out and achieve them.

Chapter 7

Social Policy Bonds, policymaking and policymakers

This chapter discusses looks at how the Social Policy Bonds, with their focus on outcomes rather than activities or institutions, would first interact with, and then reshape, the current policymaking environment. It concludes with a brief look at how the bonds could be used to solve social and environmental problems in developing countries.

Government spending in the developed countries amounts to an average of 46 per cent of Gross Domestic Product. Much of the debate about this spending centres around its size, rather than its inefficiency. Yet the two are linked: it is hard to voice the case for reducing the size of government when many social problems persist. And these problems persist, I believe, because the government programmes that aim to tackle them reward doing, rather than achieving. People are paid for their time, rather than their efficiency or success. As a result, government programmes are cumbersome and inefficient. Typically they are unresponsive to events and lack ability to adapt to local circumstances. There is no incentive for the people who run them to do so efficiently. Even worse, some programmes have perverse incentives: if a police force, for example, is too successful at cutting crime one year, it may find its budget cut the following year. Or at least, the possibility that this might happen could have some effect on performance.

Social Policy Bonds, on the other hand, would be explicitly focused on outcomes. As such, they would command wider political support than activity-based programmes. And because they inject incentives into all stages necessary for solving social problems, they will be more efficient than current efforts.

Who is likely to oppose Social Policy Bonds, and who will support them?

The main opponents are likely to come from the public sector; that is those who, facing very limited competition, supply services that would be made contestible under a Social Policy Bond regime. Other opponents could be those who believe they benefit from the current array of transfers and subsidies. There are many in industry and, as we saw in Chapter 2, in agriculture, who would suffer from the removal of their special privileges, at least in the short term. Many of these privileges are granted only because the identity of the people who receive them, and their true costs to everyone else, are not widely known. Import barriers are a prime example of policies that benefit the few at the expense of the many in ways that are not obvious to most people.

Opposition might also come from those who would be surprised to learn that they are net beneficiaries of lavish taxpayer subsidies that deliver far more to the better off than to the poor and disadvantaged. Car drivers, or rail passengers, for example, could find that they would receive little direct benefit from government funds under a Social Policy Bond regime, which would have explicit objectives that command wide support. But it is important to remember that a bond regime would probably lead to leaner, more efficient government, with consequently lower taxes. Current recipients of taxpayers' largesse might lose their subsidies, but many would have more disposable income.

It's also likely that there would be opposition from civil servants and others who administer all these transfers and subsidies. Many of these jobs would disappear during the transition to a Social Policy Bond regime, but of course there would be more, and more fulfilling jobs, created in a Social Policy Bond environment.

Public sector trade unions could be expected to resist Social Policy Bonds, as they generally have opposed privatisation or voucher schemes. Not all the opposition that has been seen to privatisation has been entirely self-seeking. There are genuine concerns arising from the fact that private companies would be the ones deciding on eligibility for state benefits, and they would have an incentive to minimise the number of eligible clients. Under a Social Policy Bond regime I do not envisage that eligibility for government benefits should ever be given to the private sector. Bondholders would have to work within the assurances that government gives about its eligibility requirements and other criteria that would affect the bond price. Eligibility would always remain a government function.

Politicians may also oppose Social Policy Bonds, despite the likelihood that the Bonds could achieve their stated objectives more readily. This opposition would come from a natural desire to hold on to power, including the policy instruments that a Social Policy Bond regime would transfer to the private sector.

However, support for Social Policy Bonds would come, I should imagine, would those who are sincere in their wish to see improvements in the position of the poorest members of society—and many politicians do fall into this category. These people would concentrate their energies on promoting the use of Social Policy Bonds that target the well-being of their constituents.

More support for Social Policy Bonds would come from who already have some experience of contracting for the public sector. In general, the poor, and those who claim to represent them would support the Bonds—if they were open-minded, and after experimental trials of the bonds had been shown to work. Crucially, all taxpayers should benefit from the lower taxes that would be likely to result from more efficient government, and unless they felt that they benefit more from the privileges they are granted under current arrangements, they are likely to support Social Policy Bonds for that reason.

Remember though that the bonds will create incentives for people to get together and solve social problems. They will have their own dynamic and create their own interest groups, whose overriding interest will not necessarily *be* the public interest, but will certainly *coincide with* it. The effects of creating such interest groups will be incalculable.

Efficiency and transparency—a potent combination

Social Policy Bonds would combine efficiency in achieving social goals with transparency about what these goals are, and how much they will cost. I have discussed each quality separately. But the combination of the two would transform policymaking. Gone would be much of government's discretion as to which interest groups receive this or that amount of public spending. The thrust of political debate would shift away from discussion about policy instruments and spending as a measure of commit-ment to achieving social goals. Instead it would concentrate on:

- consultation with voters as to what society's goals should be;
- seeking, and articulating, information as to the trade-offs that are involved in achieving particular social goals;

- defining society's goals in terms that people can understand and that are measurable; these goals would be explicit and would appear on election manifestos—their relative priority would be a matter for open political debate; and
- organising the issue of Social Policy Bonds, and their redemption, when satisfied that the redemption conditions had been met.

Government would still have some discretionary powers to allocate finance to meet unexpected events. Initially at least there would be some public services, such as defence, where outcomes are difficult to define and quantify. But its almost total discretionary power over 46 per cent of GDP would be gone, probably for ever. Naturally this would be hard for government to contemplate. But it is, I believe, necessary: there are too many obsolete, redundant, dysfunctional or counterproductive government programmes, and they are responsible for a great deal of resource misallocation.

Government though would benefit to the extent that people would not automatically blame it if things were not achieved. And the fact that Social Policy Bonds specify explicit outcomes, and achieves them efficiently would allow government to tackle issues that are best dealt with at a national level, but have been neglected. I am thinking particularly of the environment, where Environmental Policy Bonds would be a better alternative, I believe, than regulation or taxes or such other market-based ideas as tradeable permits to pollute. The outcome-orientation of Social Policy Bonds could make government less wary about stipulating goals too in other areas, such as crime, where there is consensus over what result is required, but little agreement on how to get there. In the future, after the Bonds have been used and accepted, it may be that people will want to widen their scope so that they target what are today nebulous ideas, such as 'happiness' or 'community'. More likely they will want to restrict the objectives targeted by Social Policy Bonds, and thus the role of government, to easily quantifiable goals that address either the problems of the disadvantaged or those concerns like the environment that are genuinely in the nature of a public good.

Most likely then, government would be smaller than it is now. There would be many benefits from a smaller, more efficient government that solved social and environmental problems by issuing Social Policy Bonds. Apart from doing a better job of looking after the poorest members of society directly, smaller government, and a reduced tax burden would have further benefits:

1. Lower taxes reduce the burden to the economy by more than the taxes themselves. This is only partly because of savings in the administration costs that taxes impose. More important are the so-called deadweight costs of taxes. These arise because of the way taxes distort production and consumption behaviour. They mean that even if all tax revenue were handed straight back to producers and consumers, the economy as a whole would be worse off than if there were no taxes. Deadweight losses would be much reduced in a lower-tax environment.

2. Tax cuts have acquired something of a bad name in recent years, and there is no question that the major beneficiaries of income tax cuts have been the rich. But it is important to realise that under a bond regime the poor would benefit not only from more efficient provision of services currently supplied by government, but also from future tax cuts. Most low income earners pay proportionately high marginal tax rates, paying as they do, both income taxes and social security taxes. Their employers are also likely to be paying a payroll tax. While a general cut in taxes would benefit the already wealthy, the poor would also gain significantly.

Many people object to big government not only on the grounds that it is inefficient, incompetent or worse, but on the grounds that it infringes the liberty of its citizens, by virtue of size alone. For these people, smaller government would be an end in itself.

Social Policy Bonds and developing countries

I have discussed Social Policy Bonds as if they would be applied only in developed countries. This has mostly been because the size of the public sector in developed countries is bigger than in the developing countries, and also because these countries' government policies, and their performance are better documented. I believe, though, that Social Policy Bonds would, in many ways be at least as well suited to application in developing countries. There are several reasons for this:

- Public sectors are growing even faster in developing countries than in the developed world from, of course, a smaller base. There is the opportunity therefore to avoid the mistakes that developed countries made when their public sectors grew.
- While public sectors in the developing countries are growing rapidly, they are still not big enough to cope with their very severe social problems and the enormous social changes that are occurring. Developing countries are urbanising rapidly, with all the social dislocation this entails. Crime rates are high, and there is a great deal of urban poverty and unemployment. Many children are outside the educational system altogether, and standards in the state system, while variable, are generally very low. Environmental problems are especially severe in developing countries.
- Public sector employees in developing countries are generally not well paid, and are more susceptible to corruption than in most developed countries. This makes them even

less well motivated to act in the public interest. As in developed countries, there is often little relationship between government spending and desirable outcomes. So a recent IMF working paper can conclude, after surveying 50 developing countries that 'there is little empirical evidence to support the claim that public spending improves education and health indicators'.[28]

Despite their smaller government infrastructure, there is no reason why governments in developing countries could not issue Social Policy Bonds and redeem them. They could target broad health, educational and environmental objectives, where improvements could come quite rapidly, and whose achievement could bring financial benefits to the government that could easily outweigh financial costs. It is likely that efforts at data collection in most countries would probably have to be strengthened, but that would be a far less daunting task than enlarging what, in many cases, is a corrupt and incompetent public sector and trusting in it to achieve social objectives.

Unfortunately, even more than in the rich countries, the stated objectives of politicians and governments, differ from their real intentions. In many developing countries powerful politicians use their own hidden networks of placemen in key positions in important ministries to frustrate whatever projects or policies they find inconvenient. Outsiders, including especially overseas aid donors, find little correlation between what the governments in these countries say they want and what they do. World Bank

---

28. *Does higher government spending buy better results in education and health care?*, Anjeev Gupta, Marijn Verhoeven and Erwin Tiongson, IMF Working Paper WP/99/21,

and IMF personnel officially judge countries on their stated policies and plans, but in many countries these bear little relationship
to the way the country is actually run.[29]

It may be that, in time, aid to these countries could be used to
redeem Social Policy Bonds, instead of being given on a govern-
ment-to-government basis, thereby bypassing corrupt politicians
and officials, and the institutions they control. Funds aimed at
solving global environmental problems, such as climate change,
could similarly reward those who undertake worthwhile projects,
rather than corrupt governments (see chapter 5). Or, corrupt
governments could choose to buy globally-backed bonds. Their
financial self-interest would dictate their modifying their behaviour in favour of targeted global goals.

---

29. 'Africa: the heart of the matter', *The Economist*, 13 May 2000.

Chapter 8

Putting it all together

From 'Letters to the Editor', *The Times*, London, 14 August 1999:

Yesterday I was told by my doctor that she cannot, at present, refer patients suffering from varicose veins for hospital treatment. Today I read your report that hospital waiting lists have come down. Is this coincidence? Are patients with complaints which, while not life-threatening are extremely irritating and debilitating, being denied treatment so that the Government can maintain that it has fulfilled an election pledge?

Indeed. This chapter first looks at some objectives of recent local and central government initiatives in the UK, and at how they, and their associated indicators, could be improved and targeted by Social Policy Bonds. Then I look in more detail at the financial benefits of targeting objectives with Social Policy Bonds. Finally, I discuss how objectives should be decided, and suggest a range of broad social objectives that would suit a Social Policy Bond regime.

Ends, or means to ends?

Earlier, we said that objectives should be broad, carefully defined, and adequately represented by one or a group of quantifiable indicators. The distinction between objectives and indicators is not always clear—it is usually a matter of degree.

Some 'indicators' currently in use can amount to little more than a means to an end; the sort of indicator—such as money spent on a problem, or person-hours devoted to solving it—that could have little or no correlation with actual achievement of the objective it supposedly represents. Their use bedevils government programmes the world over.

A Social Policy Bond regime needs indicators that either are, or are very closely correlated with, the actual objective. The reason for this is simple. When bonds are issued, people are not told *how* to achieve a targeted objective. So the ways in which they try to achieve it cannot be assumed. This means that if a targeted objective is just a means to an end, it may be that the bonds could be redeemed without the actual end being achieved.

This need for an indicator that either is, or is very closely correlated with, the actual objective limits the applicability of a Social Policy Bond regime, as much as it does the role of government in a complex society. Even under the current system, in which objectives are not targeted by means of Social Policy Bonds, it is preferable for them to be represented by indicators that are as close as possible to the actual objective. Otherwise there is greater scope for manipulation of the data. Our ultimate objectives are inescapably subjective. We want happiness or, as a society, we want what economists call social welfare. We can't measure either of those qualities, but we can still improve on some indicators that are being proposed for use. I shall look at examples from two main sources:

1. Cheshire County Council's Target 2000 indicators

Cheshire is a county in north-west England, bordering on North Wales with a population of around 670 000. The Cheshire County Council ('CCC') is the county's local authority, and is responsible for a wide range of activities. In mid 1999 it issued a list of its targets in a small, widely distributed pamphlet called *Target 2000*.[30] Where my comments are negative they are not meant to be an indictment of the CCC. The indicators in *Target 2000* are not definitive, and the CCC did well to publish and seek feedback on them. There is no suggestion either that they would be targeted by Social Policy Bonds.

2. New Labour's *Opportunity for All*

In September 1999 Britain's Government released a 168-page report, *Opportunity for All—Tackling Poverty and Social Exclusion*,[31] its first annual audit of the state of poverty in Britain. Alistair Darling, the Social Security Secretary, hailed the report as a landmark in the campaign against poverty, which reflected the changing nature of the welfare state. He said: 'For the first time a Government is standing up to be counted, setting specific standards against which we will be judged.' *Opportunity for All* lists 49 'key initiatives' aimed at tackling poverty and social exclusion. These are not new policies, but what *is* new, and deserves attention, are the Government's 38 indicators of poverty, against which it says it will measure its progress. Its objectives, initiatives and 'indicators of success' look at deprivation under four headings. We shall concentrate on the indicators.

I comment on indicators under the headings education, mental health, physical health, environment, crime and transport, but these do not always correspond to the headings used in the sources.

---

30. Target 2000, Cheshire County Council, 1999
31. *Opportunity for All—Tackling Poverty and Social Exclusion*, The Poverty and Social Exclusion Team, Department of Social Security, 1-11 John Adam Street, London WC2N 6HT, September 1999

Education

One of New Labour's 1997 election manifesto commitments was to bring class sizes for five-, six-and seven- year olds down to a maximum of 30. Is this a useful indicator? The question is whether smaller class sizes are an end in themselves, or whether they are only loosely correlated with what society wants; presumably, better education. If society merely wants improved, measurable, educational outcomes, then it would be better to target educational achievement directly, rather than class sizes. But we should be open-minded as to whether there are other, unspecified, benefits of smaller class sizes. It may be that smaller class sizes *are* seen as a valuable end in itself. If so, or if smaller class sizes are closely correlated to a less easily measured objective, such as more attention paid per pupil, then it is worthwhile targeting smaller class sizes in their own right.

New Labour's more recent education commitments for young people, as described in *Opportunity for All* include:

> *Ensuring that all children get a high-quality education wherever they go to school and providing additional help to children in the crucial pre-school years*

Future policy milestones

> *At least 250 local Sure Start[32] programmes in England by 2001/02 and 100 per cent of families in contact with the local Sure Start programmes within the first two months of the birth of the child*

---

32. In April 1999 the first 21 'Sure Start' programmes were announced in areas of England where children are judged to be most at risk from poverty and social exclusion. They offer help to families with children from birth up to the age of four.

To expand early years education provision for three-year-olds across the UK
Continued roll-out of Education Action Zones[33]
Maths Year 2000[34]

Indicators of success

An increase in the proportion of seven-year-old Sure Start children achieving level 1 or above in the Key Stage 1 English and maths tests.

An increase in the proportion of those aged 11 achieving level 4 or above in the Key Stage 2 tests for literacy and numeracy.

A reduction in the proportion of truancies and exclusions from school.

An increase in the proportion of 19-year-olds with at least a level 2 qualification or equivalent.

This, to my mind, is excellent. Policy milestones are explicit and expressed in such a way that we can know whether they have been met or not. The 'indicators of success' appear right below the policies: the people involved in the policies know exactly how their effectiveness will be measured. And the indicators are sensible. The educational indicators concentrate on basic educational achievement in literacy and numeracy. Exclusion from school, whether by truancy or expulsion, is rightly targeted: it is a problem in itself, and the cause of problems in later life. The last indicator, applying to 19-year olds, is not overly ambitious.

---

33. Each Zone receives public and private sector funding of up to £1 million a year for a period of three or five years.

34 'Maths Year 2000' aims to reinforce teachers' efforts in the classroom by involving parents, business and the wider community and helping people of all ages to improve their skills in maths.

Further educational objectives given in *Opportunity for All* are:

A reduction in the proportion of 16-18-year-olds not in education or training.

An improvement in the educational attainment of children looked after by local authorities.

Less rigorous are *Target 2000*'s educational indicators:

Lifelong learning

Number of nursery education places available to three year olds

This is a good as an objective, but if bonds were issued, the words 'for each 1000 three year olds in Cheshire', or something similar, would have to be added, to guard against too many places being available if there were a fall in the number of three year olds. Also the word 'available' would need to be defined. It is possible that the better off would be the major beneficiaries of a policy of increasing nursery numbers, but it is also arguable that, even so, there is a large public good component in expanded nursery education, and that society as a whole (and not just the pupils involved) benefits from it.

The next *Target 2000* indicators show a commendable concentration on the basics:

Percentage of 11 year olds reaching expected standard of English

Percentage of 11 year olds reaching expected standard of Maths

Percentage of 16+ with five higher grade GCSEs

Percentage of 16+ with at least one GCSE

Universal education in English and Maths can easily be seen as a public good, and these are good indicators. The role of the local authority becomes more questionable with the next objective:

Number of sixth formers achieving two A levels (or equivalent) and their average points score

The problem is one of priorities. Should council funding be used to raise the qualifications of the already relatively-bright? This funding will have to come from some other claim on the budget. There would still be a substantial public good element in sixth form education, but less so than at a more basic level. There are no easy answers, but a Social Policy Bond regime would at least make educational priorities and trade-offs a matter for consultation and debate.

Mental health

Some of health objectives and indicators in *Target 2000* appear less robust:

One of them, for example, is

To cut the number of emergency psychiatric hospital re-admissions

Probably, the words 'per total number discharged' are to be understood at the end of it, but even so, it does not appear to be a legitimate objective. The danger is that it could be achieved simply by making it more difficult for patients to leave hospital, regardless of how likely they are to need to be readmitted. It could also be achieved by refusing to admit anyone, except either those who are unlikely ever to be released, or those who are judged to be in so little need of treatment that they perhaps shouldn't be admitted in the first place. That said, finding indicators of mental health is no easy matter. Verifiable quantitative measures of success are particularly difficult to envisage in this area, because of the subjective nature of our mental experience. One approach is to target 'access' indicators, such as the availability of counseling services, or places in psychiatric hospitals. These are more in the nature of outputs than outcomes. Of course, the problem of measuring the effectiveness of policy in mental health is not unique to a Social Policy Bond regime. And because even the outcomes that I have suggested be targeted, such as physical health, the environment, crime and pollution, are only means to an end that is ultimately subjective, neither is it unique to mental health. I shall say more on the limits of quantifiable indicators in my final chapter.

Physical health

From *Target 2000*:
Cutting the number of:
...children placed on the Child Protection register
emergency admissions to hospital of people over 75 years
...unnecessary admissions, or inappropriate placements or discharge of older people admitted to hospital

I don't think these are sound indicators. There may be an increase in the *need* for Child Protection, or for emergency hospital admissions. Reducing numbers would not be legitimate under such circumstances. The third indicator would be acceptable, if the words 'unnecessary' and 'inappropriate' could be adequately defined, but that would appear unlikely. Many admissions or placements would be known to be 'unnecessary' only after admission to hospital. How would these be classed?

Also from *Target 2000*:
To help young people resist drug misuse.
Cutting the number of accidents among young people and older people
To cut by one third the number of people killed or seriously injured [on the roads] by 2010

Drug abuse by young people is a serious problem. It doesn't follow that a local authority, or any authority, will have much success in solving it. Should the local authority therefore do nothing?

Not necessarily. If it has an allocation for health spending, it should use it in ways that maximise its return. That may mean targeting drug abuse among young people, but it could mean targeting under-age driving, or a host of other higher priorities. If drug abuse among young people were to be targeted, it would be very difficult to find a reliable indicator: what is given here is not an indicator, but an objective. Possible indicators of drug abuse could come from surveys of police, parents or schools.

The accident indicators could run into definitional problems. It is not clear what sort of accidents are to be measured: all accidents, or serious accidents, or reported accidents? Lax reporting, or a phone permanently off the hook, could lead to a reduction in the latter, and anyway the role that a local government authority has to play in accident prevention is probably limited.

It would be difficult to find reliable indicators for either drug abuse or accidents, but it is not simply because relevant indicators would be difficult to find that targeting accidents or drug abuse is questionable: it is by no means certain that a rational health policy would focus on either accidents or drug abuse, even though they have a high public profile. A Social Policy Bond regime would target general health indicators, such as longevity, infant mortality or the mortality rates for different age, sex or racial groups, and it may be that treating drug abuse and accidents as special cases would be inefficient, in that greater health benefits could be gained by concentrating resources in other areas. Much, of course, will depend on the precise definition of targeted health outcomes, and one argument in favour of targeting road accidents and drug abuse is that they fall particularly hard on young people. It may be rational policy to place a higher priority on the health of young people than others, and if an indicator such as longevity is thought not to give the health of younger age groups a high enough priority, then an indicator such as the 'life expectancy of people below the age of 30' may be chosen. Even then, though, it would be best if government didn't decide in advance what it thinks are the best ways of helping young people live longer. It may well be that holders of bonds targeting the longevity of under 30-year olds decide to target drug abuse or road accidents, but they may also find other ways of increasing the benefit to young people for each taxpayer's dollar.

For the youngest, though, needs are more immediate and less equivocal:

From *Opportunity for All*:

Health outcomes in Sure Start areas:

> —*a reduction in the proportion of low birth-weight babies in Sure Start areas; and*
> —*a reduction in the rate of hospital admissions as a result of serious injury in Sure Start areas.*

Low birth weight and serious injuries are easily measured and do correlate with poverty and social deprivation. Serious injuries, however caused, indicate violence and danger. Both these indicators are correlated with what society wants to achieve.

Teenage pregnancy:

> —*a reduction in the rate of conceptions for those aged under 18; and*
> —*an increase in the proportion of those....teenage parents [who are], in education, employment or training.*

Again, the goal is sound, and the indicators are well chosen. Britain has the highest rate of teenage pregnancies in Western Europe. This is both a symptom and a cause of poverty: fewer than half of single mothers of children aged five to 11 have jobs, while many of those not working do not appear on official unemployment statistics because they are not looking for work.

Environment

From *Target 2000*:

Increasing the percentage of household waste used for recycling

There is real confusion here. 'Recycling' has been taken to be an end in itself, but it should not be. If the aim is to improve the environment, then it is not at all certain whether more recycling will do that. There are environmental costs in recycling too, and for most products, and in most circumstances (because location can be important too), whether recycling something has a bigger negative impact on the environment than using the same thing just once or not is open to question. Recycling a glass bottle, say, means using additional energy to clean the bottle and to sterilise. It means manufacturing, transporting and disposing of the detergent. To show that recycling say a glass bottle, rather than disposing of it, and using a new one, is better for the environment, one would have to show that all the environmental costs in these, and other, additional processes are lower than for disposing of the old bottle and manufacturing a new one. This is a difficult thing to prove, even at a single point in time. And technologies and therefore environmental costs and benefits also change. They also differ according to such variables as location. Some households, for example, may be sited right next to a recycling plant and that could be enough to tip the environmental balance in favour of recycling—for those households. Few 'life cycle analyses', which compare all the environmental costs and benefits of recycling with the alternative, have been done, and those that have do not show unequivocal evidence in favour of recycling on environmental grounds. One life cycle analysis estimated that the manufacture of paper cups consumed 36 times as much electricity and more than 500 times as much wastewater as the manufacture of much-derided polystyrene foam cups.[35] Another study found that while disposable nappies create around two times as much trash by volume as recyclable cloth nappies, they are probably more friendly to the environment, consuming less energy than, and half as much water as, cloth nappies. They also generate 40 per cent less air pollution, and 86 per cent less water pollution.[36]

Rather than aim for recycling then, it would be far better to target environmental pollution directly. Environmental Policy Bonds could do this by targeting some or all of a combination of pollution indicators, including:

nationally averaged indices of pollution, weighted according to lethality, taken at sites throughout the country, and comprising proportions of noxious air and water pollutants;

- numbers of people found in surveys to be suffering from respiratory ailments;
- responses of residents and overseas to questions about their perception of the environment.

From *Target 2000*:
Cutting our electricity, gas and oil consumption by 15 per cent between 1998 and 2003, based on consumption levels for 1997.

---

35. *Paper versus polystyrene: a complex choice*, Martin B Hocking, Science 251, pp 504-5, 1 February 1991.

36. *Energy and environmental profile analysis of children's disposable and cloth diapers*, Franklin Associates Ltd, Prairie Village, KS, USA, July 1990.

The principle of tackling all the major causes of pollution at once is sound, but I believe that the pollution consumption of electricity, gas and oil generates is best dealt with by targeting nationally averaged pollution indices, as described above. The CCC could, though, target pollution levels in Cheshire by rewording its objective as: 'cutting our average air pollution by 15 per cent....' There are other deficiencies with the original objective. If the Cheshire population expands, or if new industries move into the county, consumption of electricity, oil and gas will be likely to rise. Does the local authority want to deter industries relocating to Cheshire? If not, the objective would be better expressed as 'Cutting the average electricity, gas and oil consumption *per household* by 15 per cent....' That still leaves the question of what would happen if there are some exceptionally cold winters. For a similar reason it's also unwise to choose one year as a base. The average of three years (1995-97, say) would be more representative.

Transport

Much publicity accrues to road congestion, and much of the policy rhetoric is aimed at freeing up the roads. Thus, from Target 2000, under the header *Cutting traffic jams:*

To cut the 35 per cent predicted rise in traffic growth by 2011 by more than half

The question is whether road congestion is a symptom of a problem, a problem in itself, or nothing at all to worry about. What is the problem with traffic jams? The people who are in them prefer to be in them than to take public transport. People have choices about how they get to work, or where they work. There is a real danger that 'cutting traffic jams' will be used to justify more road building. Or that 'cutting the predicted rise in traffic growth...' will lead to more subsidies for public transport.

This is the sort of public spending that would almost certainly become a subsidy from the poor to the rich. We need to be clear what the real objective is here. Is it to reduce average commuting time? If so, that could be targeted directly, though I suspect that such an objective would also involve transfers from the poor to the better off. If better air quality is the real objective, then I suggest targeting air pollution directly, and letting the private sector take the initiative in road management.

As with road building, so with public transport. *Target 2000* gives as one of its objectives, under the header 'Improving public transport'

To provide a twice daily bus service to 80 per cent of rural villages.

This could be worded better: it doesn't tell us how many villages already receive such a bus service. Perhaps 80 per cent would represent a decline? Also, the word 'provide' should be replaced 'ensure', as bus services can be contracted out. A better indicator altogether might target *usage* of public transport. Even then, though, the better off tend to be the bigger beneficiaries of such programmes. There's nothing necessarily wrong with subsidising the bus trips of the middle class, but it would seem an odd priority given the other challenges that local authorities have to confront.

My own view is that under an outcome-orientated policymaking system, both central and local government in the developed countries would have little to do providing services or new infrastructure. Better transport may be an urgent need for some people and families, but the problem for many of them is lack of funds for their own vehicles or for public transport. Bondholders targeting indicators addressing such objectives as employment, health (including mental health) or education would address the transport needs of these people.

General comments

Target 2000 includes other indicators such as:
Number of visits per head of population to public libraries and
Percentage of draft educational needs statements [for people with special needs] prepared within 18 weeks

In a Social Policy Bond regime, it would be more efficient, as well as simpler, to subsume such micro-objectives into larger ones. So the 'library visits' objective would be subsumed under general educational objectives, while objectives targeting acceleration of administrative procedures would be jettisoned. But even under the current regime, there are dangers, which I have briefly mentioned, in targeting such indicators as those on emergency psychiatric re-admissions. It is possible to anticipate many ways in which they can be manipulated or abused, but experience will also be valuable.

Target 2000 shows that many fine-sounding objectives can easily become a means by which the poor would end up subsidising the middle class or the rich, whether they be car-drivers, public transport users, the wealthy parents of bright children of wealthy parents or whoever. Social Policy Bonds, would concentrate on a smaller number of broad objectives, specifying outcomes that are unambiguously helpful. The law of diminishing returns suggests that the best returns, measured as benefit per unit outlay, will go to those bondholders who help those who are least able to help themselves. While there is arguably nothing wrong with a system that takes money from the poor, and transfers it to the better off, such a policy programme has never been explicit in any election manifesto, and the fact is that nobody does attempt to justify such transfers. They occur by default, because of a confused and opaque policymaking process.

Opportunity for All is better. Apart from the indicators cited, others aim for reductions in the proportion of children living in workless households, or in households with low relative and absolute incomes, or suffering fuel poverty. All these are sound indicators—though it is more defensible to define poverty in terms of low absolute incomes rather than low relative incomes.

Some have criticised *Opportunity for All* because of its 38 indicators of poverty. 'With so many measures, what will count as success?' asks *the Economist*[37], 'different indicators may point in different ways'. It is difficult to see what *would* satisfy the journal given that in the same article it says that it is impossible to find a single measure of poverty, 'which has many facets'. But the opposition Conservatives echoed this criticism, accusing the Government of being in a 'damaging muddle' about the issue. David Willetts, the shadow social security spokesman, said: 'In setting out so many poverty indicators the Government will be tempted to tackle them all at once without solving any of them.'[38] Again, it is hard to think what would satisfy the opposition.

The Child Poverty Action Group said the strategy did not go far enough, and it urged Government to repudiate any further tax cuts and give a commitment to reducing inequalities in incomes, health and education[39] Its director said: 'Setting targets for reading are (sic) no good if a child living in poverty is living in a cold, unheated home.' In truth, the proportion of households with children living in 'fuel poverty' *is* one of the targeted indicators; as is relative inequality. The CPAG is also saying that rejecting tax cuts is an end in itself!

---

36. 'Labour's crusade', *The Economist*, 25 September 1999, page 72.
37. *Daily Telegraph*, 22 September 1999.
38. *Daily Telegraph*, 22 September 1999.

The relevance of all this for Social Policy Bonds is twofold:

1. A great deal of thinking has gone into defining these 38 indicators in *Opportunity for All*. Quibbles about the merits of targeting relative poverty aside, the indicators are sound: they are explicit, transparent and quantifiable. They show that even the existing political process can generate meaningful and valuable indicators.

2. The current British Labour Government has said that it is prepared to be judged on what happens to these indicators. It is heartening to read the Government saying early on in the report that 'We are determined to make a difference and we are prepared to be judged on our results.'

Both these facts bode well for acceptance of policy that targets outcomes, such as a Social Policy Bond regime.

Of course, I have my own criticisms, not of the individual indictors appearing in *Opportunity for All*, but of how the British Government will target them:

- the desired outcomes refer only to the direction of movement of the targeted indicators, not to the magnitude of this direction, so that

- it will be impossible to know whether the objectives are being achieved efficiently, especially as the people charged with achieving the targeted objectives will face little competition from other bodies.

Opportunity for All does mention the costs of many of the programmes mentioned in the report. Not all these costs are as transparent as they could be, very clear. But let us take as an example the numeracy and literacy objectives, whose costs are made clear:

'Funding of £120 million a year for the next three years has been supplemented this year by a further £48 million to help pupils who have fallen behind. In addition, since taking office in 1997, the Government has given schools a total of £115 million to spend on books.'[39]

Even if the literacy and numeracy indicators move in the right direction it is impossible, with only this information, to know how whether the Government is getting good value for the taxpayers' funds. This is because even if the proportion of seven and 11 year olds achieving the required standards rising by just a fraction of a percentage point, the Government will be able to say that it has succeeded. The millions of pounds devoted to this objective may bring about such a tiny proportionate rise—but if they were better spent they might achieve a much bigger increase. We shall never know, because there will be no real incentives for people to spend these sums efficiently, and nobody competing with them to make sure they do so.

This failing, an important one, applies to most government activity. So, despite *Opportunity for All*'s welcome openness about costs and desired outcomes, it does not go far enough. We do know, and it is helpful, that because the Government has publicised its indicators widely, it will do its best to move them in the right direction. But even if all its objectives are achieved, we shall never know whether the Government's programmes are excellent value for money, or another colossal waste of taxpayer funds.

Cost and efficiency

Social Policy Bonds are costed, which means that the maximum cost of achieving any objective is known in advance.

---

39. Opportunity for All, chapter 3, para 18.

The Cheshire County Council in *Target 2000* gives no indication of the cost of achieving its objectives. The UK Government in *Opportunity for All,* gives the costs of many of its programmes, but does not give the targeted magnitude of the changes in its indicators. So we should have no idea whether the Cheshire County Council is achieving its goals simply by diverting funds from other objectives that aren't mentioned in the *Target 2000.* And we shall have no idea whether the British Government is making real inroads into poverty, or spending the allocated millions of pounds on fractional percentage point improvements. In neither the Cheshire County Council's nor in the Government's case shall we know whether performance, measured as the improvement in indicator per taxpayer's pound, is excellent or dreadful or anything in between. This may be good politics, but it is bad economics.

Costing of objectives under a Social Policy Bond regime

It is easy to criticise, and I haven't had the misfortune of inheriting outmoded management systems. So how would a Social Policy Bond regime cost its objectives? Simple. The market would do it.

Targeting definite, quantified objectives ensures that the government is not in the dark when trying to assess the financial cost of achieving a certain objective. Let us take the example of literacy for 11 year olds in the UK, which currently stands at 63 per cent.[40] Say that 1 million Social Policy Bonds, redeemable for £10 each, are issued targeting an achievement level of 68 per cent, and

---

40. This figure is the 'proportion of those aged 11 meeting the standard of literacy for that age', taken from the UK Government's Annual Report 1998/99, July 1999, Cm 4401, page 11. The Government is aiming to increase this proportion to 80 per cent by 2002.

floated on the market. The maximum cost to the government of achieving this objective is then £10 million. But if the bonds, when issued, fetch £5 each, then the market is saying that it thinks it can achieve this objective for just £5 million. It doesn't say *when* it thinks it can achieve that objective, but that can be inferred from market behaviour, and the market value of the bonds compared with other financial indicators. But what if the bonds sell for virtually nothing, and the market value of the bonds fails to move from that floor? That would mean that the government had miscalculated: in the market's view there is no realistic chance of the objective being achieved *for an outlay of £10 million*, in the foreseeable future. The government can respond in different ways:

- It can wait for new technology to arrive, or for circumstances to change in other ways, such that the market sees the objective as becoming more easily achievable, and the value of the bonds consequently rises. Or
- It can issue more bonds redeemable for £10. It can do this in stages, gauging the market reaction to each new tranche of bonds, which will tell government the maximum cost of achieving the objective.

Either way, the government can be reasonably sure that it is getting a good deal. But it is not only the total cost of achieving the objective that the market reveals. It is also the *marginal* cost of achieving further improvements. Say the one million bonds targeting a literacy level of 68 per cent actually sell for £5. This tells the government that the present value of the expected maximum cost of achieving an improvement of five percentage points in literacy (from 63 to 68 per cent) is £5 million. The government may therefore judge that it is well worth being more ambitious, and aim for 73 per cent literacy. So it could issue a million further bonds redeemable when literacy reaches 73 per cent. These would (probably) have a market value of less than £5, but maybe not much less, reflecting the (probably) diminishing returns involved in improving national literacy rates. The point is that, by letting the market do the pricing of the bonds, the government is getting an informed view on the marginal cost of its objectives. So if the bonds targeting 73 per cent literacy sell for £4, then the maximum cost of achieving that objective is £11 million equal to: £5 million (paid out when literacy moves from 63 to 68 per cent) plus £6 million (paid out when literacy reaches 73 per cent). The marginal cost of a five per cent increase in literacy is revealed to rise from £5 million to £6 million. Should the government go for 78 per cent literacy? Under a Social Policy Bond regime it would have some idea of the cost of doing so.

This information will be continuously updated. Say that improvements in technology, of the sort that might be stimulated by an initial literacy-targeting Social Policy Bond issue, mean that it becomes much cheaper to teach people how to read. Bondholders may have financed the creation of new literacy-teaching software, for instance. How would the market react to such a development? Once the software's effectiveness was revealed, the value of all the literacy-targeting bonds would rise. Instead of being priced at £5 and £4, the two literacy-targeting bonds might sell for £8 and £7. The cost to the government of redeeming the bonds will not change—it will remain £11 million. But the market is providing new information as to the likely cost of future improvements in literacy. Five per cent improvements in literacy now would cost £2 million (from 63 to 68 per cent), and £3 million (from 68 to 73 per cent). The new software has reduced the costs from £5 million and £6 million (respectively). So the cost of a further five per cent improvement will also fall, and the market has given its idea of approximately by how much.

These figures are invented, and simplified, but they do indicate the role that a Social Policy Bond market could play in helping the government—and the taxpayers—decide on their spending priorities.

What this section has shown is that it is not only in supplying services that the Social Policy Bonds are efficient; it is in pricing too, and for much the same reason: because pricing is not being left to government agents; the market for Social Policy Bonds is doing it, and the market has an incentive to do so efficiently.

Breadth of objective

We suggested, when looking at *Target 2000*, that targeting drug abuse amongst youths would be less efficient than targeting youth deaths or sickness generally. Similarly, why not subsume an indicator like infant mortality into longevity of the whole population? Why, in other words, target infant, or youth, mortality, separately? In fact, in efficiency terms alone, that is, in terms of extra person-years of life saved per unit outlay, it would be better to target the broader indicator. Bondholders could then allocate life-extending resources to maximise their impact on all members of society's life expectancy. This is true, so long as the 'longevity' indicator includes infants and youths in its scope. In that case, if infant deaths, or youth deaths, or deaths from road accidents, say, are to be subsumed into a 'longevity' indicator, at what level of aggregation should the process stop?

Surely what we should like ideally is a single 'quality of life' indicator, that takes into account everything: longevity, education level, environmental pollution, health level, and why not unemployment, pollution, ecological biodiversity and leisure time as well? Surely one single indicator, targeting 'social welfare' would be optimal?

There is no reason in economic logic why this could not be attempted. But there are daunting practical problems that make it inadvisable.

For the single objective of eradicating poverty, the UK Government in *Opportunity for All* is using 38 indicators. All policymaking involves making decisions on what priority certain objectives should have, but these priorities can change over time. Defining a single indicator for poverty would similarly involve subjective assessments of how the different facets of poverty affect society as a whole, but these weightings would be inflexible with time. Combining environmental goals, say, and educational goals would be even more tendentious. It would be very difficult to achieve some sort of *stable* consensus on the relative weightings attached to objectives as different as longevity and environmental pollution, to give one example. A single indicator targeting both objectives would need such a fixed ratio of weightings. Under a Bond regime, the weightings would be implied by the different sums allocated to each objective's achievement. As in the current system, government would be targeting each objective separately, so that the relative weightings could more freely change over time. Under a bond regime though, they would be the transparent outcome of a continuing political process. They could adjust according to opinion, and to changes in knowledge. For instance: if the effects of certain types of air pollution were to be proved to be more lethal than previously thought, then government could issue more bonds targeting that sort of pollution. With a highly aggregated Bond targeting some aggregate measure of 'quality of life', no such adjustment could be made. The impact of the pollutants on the quality of life would have been predetermined before the bond was issued.

Another reason for not combining many objectives into a single bond issue is the information that would be lost in doing so. Separate bond issues for literacy and birth weights gives us information about how readily each will react to targeting. This information will again be of use to policymakers.

That said, we have argued that Social Policy Bonds should not have objectives that are too narrow. To reiterate: objectives that, if not pursued jointly, could conflict—in the sense that bondholders targeting one objective could do so at the expense of another—should be targeted by a single bond issue. Applying this reasoning to the poverty indictors in *Opportunity for All*, separate bond issues would target, say, the low birth weight of babies in some areas, and literacy. But if literacy were measured as the proportion of youngsters passing literacy tests, then that indicator should be targeted by the same bond issue as truancy; otherwise the literacy indicator could rise as the number of pupils taking the test falls.

Choice of objectives

Social Policy Bonds would aim to achieve social goals efficiently. Concentrating as they do on outcomes, rather than activities, the Bonds would allow far less room for ambiguity or deception than the current system. Choice of the targeted social goals, and their associated indicators, is important for the correct working of the Bond regime. We have seen that indicators such as 'smaller hospital waiting lists' are both capable of manipulation and, even if achieved, do not necessarily correlate with what society actually wants to achieve. It would be better to target the average time between consultation and admission to hospital. But even this may be too narrow an indicator: perhaps such waiting time could be subsumed in general health objectives, such as longevity and ability to live independently and free of pain and disability.

The choice of goals is obviously going to be a matter for discussion, negotiation and constant refinement. However, I believe that objectives should fall into one or two categories.

1 Helping the poor and disadvantaged

It is no accident that the *Opportunity for All* report focuses on poverty, defined broadly. Tackling poverty and the consequences of poverty is a large part of government's *stated* rationale for supplying health, education, housing and other services. The fact that these services have largely becomes means of helping the better off, and that government is now involved in so many other activities, is largely happenstance. Government's involvement continues, though, partly through inertia, partly because it's difficult to withdraw once involved, and partly because the actual distribution of the costs and benefits of its involvement remains obscure.

A Social Policy Bond regime would change that. Its principal objectives would be to help the poorest or least disadvantaged members of society. The rationale for this is that the poor are most in need of government intervention, and also because at lower levels of real income, the correlation between a quantifiable indicator and social welfare, is a strong one. At higher levels it breaks down. Importantly, Social Policy Bonds, when targeting broad indicators as longevity, or basic educational achievement, would divert resources to where they can do most good: that is, where the maximum benefit per dollar or pound outlay can be achieved. It is those who are most disadvantaged who benefit from channeling of funds in this way. Helping the poor is the stated justification for much government intervention though, as we have seen, most of the expenditure involved doesn't actually benefit the poor. It is obvious that there is a great deal of poverty in the industrialised countries, despite taxpayers handing over large sums of their money for government programmes that were supposedly trying to eradicate it.

Suggested categories for objectives aimed at helping the poor and disadvantaged would be:

- Basic education and training
- Low unemployment —assuming that society sees employment as something more than the means to a reasonable material standard of living
- Better physical health
- Better mental health
- Numbers of homeless

Of course, by being more efficient, a Social Policy Bond regime could mean tax reductions. These would benefit the better off, who would be able to choose how to spend a higher fraction of their income.

2 Public goods

The rationale for this is the government supplying these goods cannot is that they cannot be supplied by the private sector with any efficiency. Suggested categories for goals would be:

- Law and order
- National defence
- Environmental goods

It would seem to be that in a Social Policy Bond regime, government would be smaller. When target outcomes are as transparent as they would be with Social Policy Bonds, then the panoply of measures that benefit mainly the better off will have little public support. Social Policy Bonds would also imply smaller government because government bureaucracy would be smaller. Administration costs of government programmes are notoriously high. People undertaking programmes under a Social Policy Bond regime would face similar administrative tasks, but they would do them efficiently, as they would bear these costs themselves.

Nevertheless it would be well worth discussing other possible policy areas:

Areas for discussion would be:

- Equity: is that a worthwhile goal in itself?
- Regulation: how much is necessary? Can the private sector do it more efficiently?
- International goals: alleviating poverty in the third world; peace.

There may be other things that society wishes to target, such as leisure time, or population growth rates, or self-sufficiency in certain products. I do not myself believe Social Policy Bonds should target such things, as I think they are outside the remit of government. Besides, while my list of suggested objectives appears short, it will involve many resources, and many different programmes. For instance, under the 'better physical health' heading alone, many projects could be initiated, involving such areas as accident prevention, infant mortality, cancer research and dietary advice.

Chapter 9

Government and happiness:
limits of quantifiable indicators

*'Anything that exists, exists in some quantity, and can therefore
be measured.*

Lord Kelvin[41]

Social Policy Bonds rely heavily on the use of objectives,
expressed in terms of outcomes, and targeted by quantifiable
indicators. In traditional societies, or societies where people lived
closer to each other, in every sense, people knew a lot more about
each other's general state of happiness. They knew when the people that mattered most to them were happy, and they had a fairly
good idea of what would make them happy. In our industrial
societies, with their large, complex economies, government bodies have tried to take over from extended families and local people
in supplying a range of welfare services, or the cash to pay for
them. Increasingly government is using numerical indicators,
rather than photogenic events or anecdote, to formulate policy.
And, more and more, it is these indicators that are used by the

41. quoted in Risk, John Adams, University College London Press, 1995.

media and voters to judge the success or failure of government policy, though not necessarily when casting their vote.

This use of indicators is relatively recent, unsystematic and unsophisticated. Few indicators are targeted explicitly for a sustained period: the targeted range of inflation is a rare exception, as is the coherent range of indicators presented in the British Government's *Opportunity for All* report. More commonly, other indicators—like the size of hospital waiting lists—don't measure what matters to people, or attract only fleeting attention from policymakers. One week, hospital waiting lists could come under scrutiny, the next climate change, or food safety, or road accident rates, or traffic congestion (however defined) or delays on trains or… whatever. With so many indicators, used inconsistently, incoherently, and at varying levels of aggregation, it is easy for any interest group, including politicians, to select whichever ones suit its purpose at any particular time. An indicator often used by default is the rate of growth of Gross Domestic Product. But as a single indicator of the health of an economy it is flawed: amongst other failings, it does not take into account changes in the quality of the environment, it fails to take into account the distribution of income, it ignores human capital (the education and skills that are embodied in the work force) and leisure time, and it ignores such social problems as crime and homelessness.

Even in the absence of a Social Policy Bond regime outcome-oriented, quantifiable indicators are likely to assume a greater role in policymaking. It would appear that the choice is between targeting consistent, transparent, mutually supportive indicators, and the current ad hoc arrangement that implicitly targets Gross Domestic Product along with a constantly changing, almost random, range of other indicators.

Obviously the former is better. There should be nothing frightening about this, *provided government limits its role to those areas where numbers are helpful.*

But the proviso is important. Government must recognise its limits. Government can never know as much about our happiness as real people. And Lord Kelvin's remark is false of course. Human happiness, or social welfare, *cannot* be summed up in terms of a range of quantifiable measures. Some things simply cannot be measured, and the government would do well not to get involved with them.

The future

Even if a coherent, explicit range of desirable outcomes is targeted, the question remains as to how best to achieve them. I believe, and I have tried to show, that Social Policy Bonds have significant advantages over other forms of private sector involvement, and especially over government continuing to try to achieve these goals itself.

In fact, Social Policy Bonds would blur the distinction between the public and policymakers. As the Bond concept became more widely used, people would take more of an interest in particular social and environmental goals, encouraged by the direct link between what is targeted and what is achieved. Central and local government policymaking would come under a different sort of scrutiny. People would put pressure for policy changes by looking at what is happening to outcomes. There would be no fudging. No longer would politicians be able to claim that simply by increasing expenditure in, say, health, they were addressing society's health care problems.

People would have higher expectations of what their compulsorily deducted taxes can achieve. They would take a greater interest, as political debate would discuss desired outcomes, rather than levels of funding. People would be more aware—politicians would make them more aware—of the fact that extra expenditure on, for example, keeping street crime down, might mean a worsening of local air quality. Single-issue candidates might find their messages cannot withstand such transparency.

Intra-country comparisons, already compiled in many countries, would take on new significance. People in one city or region, seeing for example, that the level of basic educational achievement of their children was lower than in other cities, might vote for more of their local taxes to reduce that disparity. They would not be discouraged by the fact that they weren't experts in the field; neither would they look to central government or educational professionals for the answer. Their focus would be on the priority they give to the educational goal as against other social goals.

At the national level, the most obscene wastes of taxpayers' money will disappear. Transfers and subsidies would be delivered to those who evidently need it. People would be given income support because they satisfied some objective criteria saying they were poor; not because they had deceived the public or played on its emotions. Wealthy farmers would lose out, and so too would producers in other sectors, who benefit (in the short term) from a wide array of other subsidies, transfers and barriers to imports, at great cost to society as a whole. Instead of allocating very large sums of money to these producers for some alleged employment benefit, government would, by issuing unemployment-targeting Social Policy Bonds, provide incentives for employment to be generated at least cost.

There would be a profound cultural effect. Politics might lose some of its adversarial edge. Political debate currently centres on allocation of expenditure (inputs) or on blame for failed achievement of outcomes. But when Social Policy Bonds become widely used it would shift towards the assessment of objective information, and the relative priorities given to different outcomes in a climate in which tradeoffs cannot be obscured.

Eventually most domestic priorities would be achieved through Social Policy Bonds.

Government employees would still supply defence services and Social Policy Bonds could not be readily be used to deal with large, unexpected civil defence emergencies—at least, not in the first years of a bond regime. Where objective criteria cannot apply, such as in cutting edge scientific research, there may also be a case for continued government involvement.

But the resulting efficiency gains from injecting self-interest into many other services currently supplied by government would take the form, I believe, of better social outcomes and lower taxes. And in a lower tax environment there will be many new opportunities. People will have more of their own money to spend, or more leisure time, or both. This can benefit people and society in many, non-monetary ways. There could be more funding for the arts; not because it is compulsorily deducted for that purpose by the government, but because people choose to spend their money on the arts themselves. Lower taxes and more leisure time mean that people can pursue more voluntary activities: helping other people, or beautifying their neighbourhoods.

Resources are always going to be limited and Social Policy Bonds will not change that. Priorities and choices will always have to be made: under the Social Policy Bond principle, governments will still decide on which problems to solve, and on the sums allocated to their solution. But democratic governments are good at representing and articulating their people's wishes. Where they are not so successful is in working out the most efficient ways of achieving these goals. This achievement is really a matter of allocating scarce resources. In economic theory, and on all the evidence, markets are the best way of allocating scarce resources to achieve prescribed ends. Social Policy Bonds would allow both governments and markets to do what each is best at doing—respectively: prescribing ends, and allocating resources to meet these ends.

In the long run the widespread acceptance of the fact that self-interest can be channeled into solving social problems could have more far-reaching implications. International transfers of taxpayer funds appear to be at least as prone to misallocation as their domestic equivalents. International, or even global, social or environmental problems, such as malnutrition or climate change, could be made the targets of future bond issues. Corrupt governments could be major purchasers of globally backed Social Policy Bonds. Or they could be paid by major bondholders to alter their policies. Either way, they would have incentives to modify their behaviour to help achieve these desired outcomes, whether these include ensuring that food supplies reach their own starving citizens, or doing what they can to achieve trans-boundary objectives such as global environmental goals. Social Policy Bonds are likely to be more effective than current aid programmes, because bondholders could benefit only by solving targeted social and environmental problems.

Internationally backed Social Policy Bonds targeting poverty, malnutrition or deadly conflicts are a long way into the future. Before we can even contemplate them, Social Policy Bonds will have to be issued on a small scale, gradually refined, and to become widely and successfully deployed at the national level.

When talking about Social Policy Bonds, I am occasionally asked whether I am serious. Handing over so much discretion as to how to achieve social goals to bondholders *does* sound outlandish, at least at first. Yet in doing so, government would not relinquish its existing sanctions against illegal acts. Government would still be defining society's goals, and it would still be the ultimate source of finance for achieving them. Any actions bondholders take would be directed toward achieving *society's* stated objectives. I believe the current system, when viewed impartially, is far more outlandish. Under it, 46 per cent of national income is being spent in pursuit of nebulous goals, few of which are costed, many of which conflict with each other, and many of which primarily benefit the better-off—some of them already very wealthy indeed. A huge bureaucracy has grown up to administer this expenditure, which, on the rare occasions its performance is even measured, it has been shown to be lamentably inefficient. With a massive public sector, and after decades of ever-increasing taxation, the British Government is today still having to target the birth weight of babies in the country's most disadvantaged areas.

The acceptance of a Social Policy Bond regime, even with the aim of achieving national goals as uncontroversial as lower crime rates, or better health and education outcomes, may be politically difficult, and must be a gradual process. But the potential benefits should not be ignored. By harnessing market forces in the service of social goals, Social Policy Bonds could, I believe, deliver better social outcomes with a smaller public sector.

Epilogue

The Social Policy Bond idea has had an unusual fate for an unusual idea. It has been in circulation for only around 12 years, so it is perhaps unsurprising that it has not been adopted anywhere, to my knowledge. But neither has it been dismissed outright. It tends to provoke initial enthusiasm amongst economists and decision makers, but then to be forgotten as other more pressing issues arise. Robert Shiller, Professor of Economics at Yale University, wrote to me at the end of 1996, praising the Social Policy Bond idea, saying that it creates "a large interest group for the solution of important problems. The political and other effects of creating such an interest group could be incalculable." An earlier draft of this book elicited extreme comments at both ends of the range: one referee called the idea "original and ingenious" and my work "a substantial contribution to debate about public policy". The other found nothing positive to say.

Some people have made interesting suggestions. Will Ware emailed me suggesting that Social Policy Bonds could be further privatised giving, as an example, infant mortality in India. Assume that it is worth a maximum of US$10,000 for a group of people to see the infant mortality rate in India drop by a third, and that these people then deposit that sum with a trustworthy agency. In return, they would receive a certificate, which they could auction for, say, US$2000. The group would lose the US$8000 difference but whoever bought the certificate would be motivated to reduce infant mortality in India. If enough people agreed on desirable objectives, and made similar deposits, the entire operation could be privatised.

My thinking, though, is that it is may be hard enough to persuade people that even the large sums at government's command can provide sufficient incentive for people actually to do anything to achieve targeted social goals. Persuading them to spend some of their after tax income on what their taxes are supposed to provide anyway would probably be more difficult than garnering support for a regime under which government undertook to redeem Social Policy Bonds.

Another idea, which keeps my original assumption of self-interested investors is to approach bookmakers: such as the people who run Britain's licensed betting offices. My idea was to ask these bookmakers a question such as 'what odds will you give me for a large bet that the crime rate will fall by 50 percent within five years?' Depending on the answer given, investors (punters) may be keen to place such a bet and do the best they can to reduce the crime rate. Or they could (subject to laws affecting bets of this nature) sell shares entitling shareholders to a fraction of the winning sum, so that these shareholders are motivated to cut crime. If enough people did this, that could constitute a fully privatised Social Policy Bond regime, though it is unlikely the bookmakers would offer favourable odds for very long.

Laurence Lau emailed me suggesting that the idea needs to framed as an experiment before it can win public support. I believe the sort of rigorous experiment he was proposing would probably be too complex and unconvincing to convert any of the unconverted, and that cautious trials by one or a few local authorities, and informal comparisons of outcomes, would demonstrate the bonds' effectiveness much more easily and almost as persuasively.

I am grateful for these, and other suggestions and comments.

www.ingramcontent.com/pod-product-compliance
Lightning Source LLC
Chambersburg PA
CBHW020240290526
45784CB00003B/1045